200 SPIRALIZER RECIPES

D0104453

HAMLYN **ALL COLOR COOKBOOK**

200 SPIRALIZER RECIPES

DENISE SMART

An Hachette UK company
www.hachette.co.uk

First published in Great Britain in 2019 by Hamlyn,
an imprint of Octopus Publishing Group Ltd,
Carmelite House, 50 Victoria Embankment
London EC4Y 0DZ
www.octopusbooksusa.com

Some of this material previously appeared in *Spiralize Now*
and *Spiralize Everyday*

Distributed in the US by Hachette Book Group,
1290 Avenue of the Americas, 4th and 5th Floors,
New York, NY 10104

Distributed in Canada by Canadian Manda Group,
664 Annette St., Toronto, Ontario, Canada M6S 2C8

ISBN 978 0 600 63590 1

A CIP catalog record for this book is available from the
Library of Congress

Printed and bound in China

1 2 3 4 5 6 7 8 9 10

Standard level kitchen cup and spoon measurements
are used in all recipes.

Ovens should be preheated to the specified temperature
—if using a convection oven, follow the manufacturer's
instructions for adjusting the time and the temperature.

Eggs should be large unless otherwise stated. This book
contains dishes made with raw or lightly cooked eggs. It is
prudent for more vulnerable people, such as pregnant and
nursing mothers, older people, babies, and young children
to avoid uncooked or lightly cooked dishes made with eggs.

This book includes dishes made with nuts and nut
derivatives. It is advisable for customers with known allergic
reactions to nuts and nut derivatives and those who may be
potentially vulnerable to these allergies, such as pregnant
and nursing mothers, the elderly, babies, and young
children, to avoid dishes made with nuts and nut oils. It is
also prudent to check the labels of packaged ingredients
for the possible inclusion of nut derivatives.

contents

introduction

introduction

A spiralizer is an affordable, easy-to-use cutting machine with a selection of blades that you can use to create a variety of different spirals, noodles, and ribbons from vegetables and fruit. It is the perfect tool if you are looking to reduce the amount of carbohydrates in your diet, and it is a great way to get more fruit and vegetables into your day-to-day meals.

Spiralizing can help you to save time, because it's really quick and easy to prepare fruit and vegetables using a spiralizer. And spiralizing can reduce cooking times, too, because many of the vegetables and fruit prepared in this way can be eaten raw or just cooked lightly, which also means that all nutrients are retained.

spiralizing & a healthy diet

A spiralizer is the ideal gadget for health-conscious cooks, because it can help you to cut back on refined carbohydrates, such as pasta and rice, by replacing them with spiralized fruit and vegetables, so you can enjoy your meals while eating fewer calories.

Carbohydrates make up an essential part of our diet and are needed for our main energy supply; they are available in three forms: sugar, starch, and dietary fiber. Some foods are high in carbohydrates, such as pasta, bread, and many processed foods, but by eating them in an unprocessed form, such as fruit and vegetables, you can absorb the best nutrients from them and eat fewer calories. A 3 oz portion (about ½ cup) of cooked spaghetti contains about 270 calories and 2 oz of carbohydrate compared to about 50 calories and ½ oz of carbohydrate for a bowl of zucchini noodles, or "zoodles," made from 1 large spiralized zucchini.

A spiralizer will encourage you to include more fruit and vegetables in your diet and can be a life-saver for those following special diets, such as low carb, gluten free, paleo, and raw food. Always check the labels of packaged ingredients if you are following a gluten-free diet to make sure they do not contain any wheat, either as an ingredient (for example, soy sauce) or through cross-contamination (for example, oats). Gluten-free versions of these products are often available and may be used instead.

Cheese is a good source of protein if you are a vegetarian, but always check the label to be sure that it is suitable for vegetarians and doesn't contain animal rennet. Some hard cheeses, such as Parmesan, and other traditional cheeses, such as Gorgonzola and buffalo mozzarella, are still made with animal rennet, although increasingly cheese is being made with "microbial enzymes" or "vegetable rennet," both of which are suitable for vegetarians. Vegetarian pasta cheese is a great alternative to Parmesan cheese, and certain cheeses, such as goat cheese, feta, ricotta, and mozzarella, are also suitable.

choosing a spiralizer

There are many brands on the market, but all essentially work in the same way. The larger horizontal and vertical ones are better for heavier root vegetables and everyday use, but small handheld ones are ideal if you are cooking for one, for occasional use, or for creating garnishes.

Spiralizers usually come supplied with a variety of blades, each of which creates a different shape. For this book, I used a horizontal spiralizer with three blades, which I have called the ⅛ inch spaghetti blade, the ¼ inch flat noodle blade, and the ribbon blade.

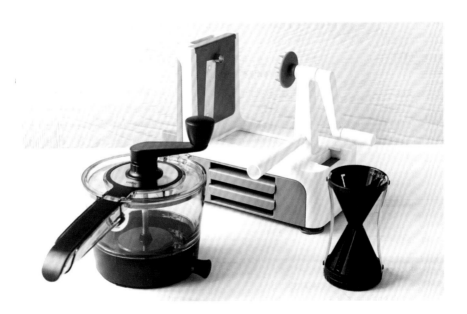

how to use a horizontal spiralizer

1 Attach the machine to the worktop using the suction feet or lever.

2 Insert the spiralizer blade you want to use into the machine.

3 Prepare the fruit or vegetable according to the recipe: peel it, if required, trim off the ends to make a flat surface, and cut in half widthwise, if necessary.

4 Attach one end of the prepared fruit or vegetable to the blade, then clamp the other end of the fruit or vegetable to the spiky grip on the crank handle.

5 Grasp the side handle for leverage, turn the crank handle, and apply a little pressure so that the fruit or vegetable is pressed between the blade and the handle—this will create spirals.

6 Finally, remove the long core and a round disk that will remain at the end of the spiralizing process.

tips for successful spiralizing

- Choose firm fruit and vegetables without pits, seeds, or hollow centers; the only exceptions are butternut squash (just use the nonbulbous end) and green papaya.

- Vegetables and fruit should not be soft or juicy; pineapples, melons, and eggplants will fall apart when you spiralize them.

- Choose vegetables that are as straight as possible. Occasionally, you may have to recenter the vegetables to avoid semicircle shapes.

- Make sure the ends of fruit and vegetables are as flat as possible by slicing a small

piece off each end. Uneven ends can make it difficult to secure the fruit or vegetable to the spiralizer and may cause them to dislodge or misalign.

- If you find that a fruit or vegetable is not spiralizing well, it may be because there is not a large enough surface area for the spiralizer to grip. For best results, pieces should be no longer than 5 inches and about 1½ inches in diameter. Cut any large vegetables in half widthwise.

- You will be left with a long core and a round disk at the end of the spiralizing process. You can save these cores to use when making soups or for snacks.

- A lot of juice is squeezed out of fruit and vegetables when you spiralize them, especially from zucchini, carrots, cucumbers, potatoes, apples, and pears. Just pat the spirals dry on paper towels before use.

- Be careful when cleaning your spiralizer, because the blades are sharp. Wash the machine in hot, soapy water and use a small kitchen brush or toothbrush to remove stubborn pieces of fruit or vegetables from the blades.

cooking tips

- Spiralized vegetables can be eaten raw or cooked quickly. The best cooking methods are stir-frying, steaming, or adding to sauces and stocks. You can also bake and roast spiralized vegetables, such as potatoes, parsnips, beets, and butternut squash in only about half the time you

would cook large chunks of the same vegetables.

- Some vegetable rices, such as beet, carrot, zucchini, and daikon radish, can be used raw. Alternatively, lightly sauté in a little oil or simmer in a little broth or sauce. They will take a short time to cook.
- It is easy to overcook vegetable spaghetti, so keep a close eye on it while cooking to make sure it doesn't fall apart.
- As a general rule, the harder the vegetable, the longer the cooking time.
- Make sauces thicker than you usually would, because certain vegetable noodles, especially ones made of zucchini, will release extra juice into your sauce.

- Pat vegetables dry on paper towels, especially zucchini and cucumbers.
- Cook your spaghetti or noodles separately, before stirring into your sauce.

storing tips

Most spiralized vegetables and vegetable rices can be stored in an airtight container in the refrigerator for up to 4 days. The exceptions are spiralized cucumber, which will keep for only about 2 days, because of its high water content, and apples, pears, and potatoes, which quickly oxidize and turn brown and so are best prepared as needed.

which fruit & vegetables can be spiralized?

I tested many different types of fruit and vegetables while writing and testing the recipes for this book. To save you wasting precious fruit and vegetables, here is a list of the ones that I found to work best.

Apples There's no need to peel or core apples, just trim the ends and spiralize whole—the core will be left behind in the machine. Spiralized apples are perfect for using in salads and savory dishes as well as desserts. Remember that the spiralized apple will turn brown quickly, so use it immediately or dress with lemon juice.

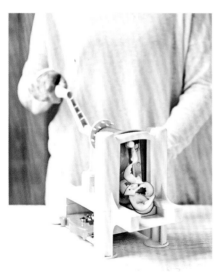

Beets There's no need to peel fresh beets, just wash the skin, flatten the ends, and spiralize whole. Eat raw in salads or bake into delicious beet chips.

Broccoli Don't throw away broccoli stems when you cook broccoli—the stems spiralizes really well. For best results, stir-fry or steam the spiralized broccoli stems.

Butternut squash To avoid the seeds, you should use only the nonbulbous end of the squash. Snip any really long strands of spiralized squash into smaller pieces using scissors—this will make the squash easier to eat.

Carrots Choose large carrots for spiralizing. Eat spiralized carrots raw in salads or steam in ribbons to create a delicious accompaniment.

Celeriac The best way to prepare this root vegetable (which is also known as celery root) is to use a sharp knife to remove the knobbly parts from the celeriac and then peel it, cut it in half widthwise, and trim to make the ends flat. Spiralized celeriac works well in gratins, soups, and remoulade.

Cucumbers Once you've spiralized the cucumber, you just need to pat the spirals or ribbons dry. Cucumbers make beautiful ribbons for using in salads.

Daikon radish Spiralized daikon radish (a long Asian radish also known as mooli) makes a great alternative to rice noodles.

Green papaya You can find green papaya in Asian grocery stores. Although it is hollow, it attaches to the spiralizer well. It is perfect eaten raw in salads.

Green plantains Choose plantains that are as straight as possible and remove the tough, outer green skin. Spiralized green plantain is delicious in curries.

Jerusalem artichokes Choose large artichokes. There's no need to peel these knobbly vegetables; all you need to do is wash them. If you're not using the spiralized artichokes immediately, put them into a bowl of water with a little lemon juice to prevent them from discolouing.

Kohlrabi Choose small kohlrabi about the size of a large apple. Prepare by peeling the outside and trimming the ends.

Onions Onions can be spiralized whole—all you need to do is trim the ends before you start. You can use spiralized onions to replace chopped ones in recipes or turn them into onion bhajis or crispy onion spirals.

Parsnips Choose large fat parsnips for the best results. Add them to hash browns or bake them to make parsnip chips.

Pears Choose firm pears for spiralizing; pears that are too ripe add too much moisture to some dessert recipes. To prepare the pears for spiralizing, just trim down the pointy ends.

Potatoes and sweet potatoes Prepare potatoes by either scrubbing or peeling, then trim the ends and cut in half widthwise, if large. Sweet potatoes are great for adding color to a dish.

Rutabagas Peel off the outside skin and cut into large chunks with flat ends to attach to the spiralizer. Use in hash browns or fritters or mixed with potatoes as a topping.

Zucchini Forget about regular pasta: spiralized zucchini make perfect "zoodles" (zucchini noodles). They can be eaten raw or lightly steamed, boiled, or stir-fried.

breakfasts

apple & blueberry pancakes

Serves **4**

Preparation time **10 minutes**

Cooking time **12–15 minutes**

2 **red apples**, ends trimmed

1¼ cups **buckwheat flour**

½ teaspoon **salt**

2 teaspoons **baking powder**

2 tablespoons **superfine sugar**

1¼ cups **buttermilk**

1 **egg**

1 cup **fresh blueberries**

1 tablespoon **sunflower oil**

To serve

handful of **blueberries**

maple syrup or **honey**

Using a spiralizer fitted with a ⅛ inch spaghetti blade, spiralize the apple.

Sift the flour, salt, and baking powder into a large bowl and stir in the sugar. Whisk together the buttermilk and egg in a small bowl. Gradually beat the buttermilk mixture into the flour to make a smooth batter. Stir in the spiralized apple and the blueberries.

Heat a large, nonstick skillet over medium heat. Dip a scrunched up piece of paper towel into the oil and carefully use it to grease the hot pan. Drop 4 large tablespoons of the batter into the pan (they will make 4 small pancakes) and cook for 2–3 minutes, until bubbles start to appear on the surface and the underside is golden brown. Flip over the pancakes and cook for another 2 minutes. Keep the pancakes warm while you cook the remaining batter, greasing the pan with a little more oil, if necessary.

Place 3 pancakes on each plate, add some blueberries with a little drizzle of maple syrup or honey, and serve.

For apple & cinnamon pancakes with blueberry compote, make the pancake batter as above, omitting the blueberries and stirring in 1 teaspoon ground cinnamon. Put 1⅓ cups blueberries into a saucepan with 2 tablespoons superfine sugar and 1 tablespoon lemon juice. Heat gently, stirring occasionally, until the blueberries start to burst and release their juice. Simmer for 2–3 minutes, until jammy. Serve the pancakes with the compote.

carrot & banana breakfast bars

Makes **16**
Preparation time **10 minutes**
Cooking time **35 minutes**

3 tablespoons **coconut** or
    olive oil, plus extra for
    greasing
3 tablespoons **date nectar** or
    honey
¼ cup **crunchy peanut butter**
2 large **carrots** (about 8 oz),
    peeled, ends trimmed, and
    halved widthwise
3 overripe **bananas**
1⅓ cups **raisins** or **golden
    raisins**
3 cups **rolled oats**

Grease an 11 x 7 inch baking pan with a little oil.

Put the date nectar or honey, peanut butter, and oil into
a small saucepan and cook over low heat, stirring from
time to time, until melted.

Meanwhile, using a spiralizer fitted with a ⅛ inch
spaghetti blade, spiralize the carrots. Coarsely snip any
really long spirals in half with a pair of scissors.

Put the bananas into a large bowl and mash them with a
fork, then stir in the spiralized carrots, raisins or golden
raisins, and oats. Pour over the peanut butter mixture
and mix well until all the ingredients are combined.

Spoon the dough into the prepared pan and flatten the
top with the back of a spoon. Bake in a preheated oven,
at 350°F, for 30 minutes, until golden brown. Remove
from the oven and let cool in the pan for 10–15 minutes.
Mark into 16 bars and let cool completely in the pan.
The breakfast bars can be stored for up to 2 days in an
airtight container.

For carrot breakfast cookies, prepare the baking
pan and 2 carrots as above. Put the carrots into a food
processor and pulse until the mixture resembles rice.
Transfer to a large bowl and add ½ cup rolled oats,
1¼ cups all-purpose flour, 1¼ teaspoons baking
power, 1 teaspoon allspice, ⅓ cup golden raisins or
raisins, 3 tablespoons coconut oil, ½ cup maple syrup,
grated zest of 1 unwaxed orange, and 3 tablespoons
orange juice. Bake in a preheated oven, at 350°F, for
15–18 minutes, until browned.

peanut butter, quinoa & apple bars

Makes **8**
Preparation time **5 minutes**,
  plus chilling
Cooking time **10 minutes**

1⅔ cups **rolled oats**
¾ cup uncooked **quinoa**
1 tablespoon **chia seeds** or
  flaxseeds
2 **red apples**, ends trimmed
½ cup **crunchy peanut butter**
½ teaspoon **sea salt**
¼ cup **honey**
2 tablespoons **apple juice**
1 tablespoon **coconut oil**

Line an 8 inch square baking pan with nonstick parchment paper.

Spread out the oats and quinoa on a large nonstick baking sheet and bake in a preheated oven, at 350°F, for 10 minutes, stirring once, or until lightly toasted. Transfer to a bowl and stir in the seeds.

Meanwhile, using a spiralizer fitted with a ¼ inch flat noodle blade, spiralize the apples.

Put the peanut butter, sea salt, honey, apple juice, and coconut oil into a saucepan and cook over low heat, stirring, until the mixture is smooth and creamy. Stir in the spiralized apples and let cool for a few minutes.

Stir the peanut mixture into the oat mixture and mix until well combined. Spoon the dough into the prepared pan and spread out evenly. Chill in the refrigerator for about 1 hour or until the mixture has hardened and set.

Remove from the pan and cut into 8 bars. The bars can be stored for up to 3–4 days in an airtight container in the refrigerator.

For quinoa porridge with spiralized pear, put 1⅓ cups cooked quinoa into a bowl, pour 1⅔ cups milk over it, cover, and place in the refrigerator for at least 2 hours or overnight. Stir in 2 tablespoons peanut butter and a little more milk, if a runnier consistency is preferred. Cut the pointy ends off 2 pears and spiralize them, using the flat noodle blade as above. Cut any really long spirals into shorter lengths with a pair of scissors, then stir into the porridge. Pour into 2 bowls and serve.

cinnamon & pear french toast

Serves **2**
Preparation time **5 minutes**
Cooking time **10–15 minutes**

1 large **pear**, pointy end
  trimmed
1 tablespoon **butter**, plus extra
  for frying
2 teaspoons packed **light
  brown sugar**

For the toast
1 extra-large **egg**
½ teaspoon **ground
  cinnamon**
1 tablespoon **superfine** or
  granulated sugar
¼ cup **milk**
2 thick slices **brioche bread**

Using a spiralizer fitted with a ribbon blade, spiralize the pear.

Melt the butter and sugar in a large skillet, add the spiralized pear, and cook over medium heat for 5–6 minutes, stirring occasionally, until lightly caramelized. Set aside.

Whisk together the egg, cinnamon, and sugar in a shallow dish, then whisk in the milk. Add the slices of bread, let soak in the mixture for a few minutes, then turn over and let stand until all the egg mixture is absorbed.

Melt a little butter in a skillet over medium heat. Add the bread and cook for 2–3 minutes on each side, until golden. Serve immediately, topped with the caramelized pear.

For honey, pear & goat cheese toast, prepare 1 pear as above, melt 1 tablespoon butter and 2 tablespoons honey in a skillet, add the spiralized pear, and cook as above. Meanwhile, toast one side of the brioche bread under a preheated hot broiler, turn over, and lightly toast the other side. Place 2 rounds goat cheese onto each slice, return to the broiler, and cook for 2 minutes or until the cheese starts to melt. Top each slice of toast with the honeyed pear and drizzle with any juices from the pan.

honey-roasted apple granola

Serves **4**
Preparation time **10 minutes,**
   plus cooling
Cooking time **35–40 minutes**

⅓ cup **honey**
2 tablespoons **coconut** or
   olive oil
2 **red apples**, ends trimmed
1⅓ cups **rolled oats**
¾ cup **white quinoa**
1 cup coarsely chopped
   whole skin-on almonds
⅓ cup **sunflower seeds**
⅓ cup **sesame seeds**

To serve
milk or **yogurt**
fresh fruit

Warm the honey and oil in a small saucepan over low heat.

Meanwhile, using a spiralizer fitted with a ribbon blade, spiralize the apples.

Put the oats, quinoa, almonds, and seeds into a large bowl, add the spiralized apples, and mix well. Pour over the warm honey mixture and stir well to combine.

Spread out the mixture on a large nonstick baking sheet and bake in a preheated oven, at 300°F, for 30–35 minutes, until golden, stirring once. Remove from the oven and let cool and harden.

Serve with milk or yogurt and fresh fruit.

For maple-roasted pear granola with pecans & berries, prepare as above, replacing the honey with maple syrup, apples with pears, and almonds with pecans. Bake as above, then remove from the oven and stir in 1 cup mixed dried berries, such as blueberries, cranberries, and cherries, and let cool and harden.

autumnal bircher muesli

Serves **2**

Preparation time **5 minutes, plus soaking**

1 small **red apple**, ends trimmed
1 small **ripe pear**, pointy end trimmed
½ cup **rolled oats**
1⅔ cups **unsweetened almond milk**, plus extra to taste
¼ cup chopped **almonds**
1 cup **fresh blackberries**

To serve
mixed seeds
maple syrup or **honey**

Using a spiralizer fitted with a ⅛ inch spaghetti blade, spiralize the apple and pear.

Put all the remaining ingredients into a large bowl, add the spiralized fruit, and stir until combined. Cover and let soak in the refrigerator for 2–3 hours, or overnight, to let the oats absorb the liquid.

Stir before serving and add a little extra milk, if a runnier consistency is preferred. Serve sprinkled with seeds and drizzled with maple syrup or honey.

For blackberry & apple oatmeal, put ¾ cup rolled oats into a saucepan with 1¼ cups almond milk, ⅔ cup water, and a pinch of salt. Simmer over low heat for 3–4 minutes, stirring occasionally, until the oats have thickened. Meanwhile, spiralize 2 apples as above. Stir the spiralized apples into the oats with ⅔ cup fresh blackberries and stir until the blackberries have softened and released their juices. Serve sprinkled with sugar or drizzled with maple syrup.

sweet potato waffles with fresh fruit

Makes **2**
Preparation time **5 minutes**
Cooking time **5–6 minutes**

1 **sweet potato** (about 8 oz),
   peeled, ends trimmed, and
   halved widthwise
1 extra-large **egg**, lightly
   beaten
scant ½ cup **buttermilk**
1 tablespoon melted **butter**
   or **coconut oil**
2 tablespoons **buckwheat
   flour**
1 teaspoon **ground cinnamon**
½ teaspoon **baking powder**
cooking spray oil or **melted
   butter**, for cooking

To serve
fresh fruit, such as
   blueberries or **raspberries**
maple syrup or **honey**

Using a spiralizer fitted with a ⅛ inch spaghetti blade, spiralize the sweet potato.

Whisk together the egg, buttermilk, melted butter or oil, flour, cinnamon, and baking powder in a large bowl. Stir in the spiralized sweet potato.

Preheat a waffle machine according to the manufacturer's directions and spray with oil or brush with a little butter. Divide the batter between the 2 waffle plates, being careful not to overfill them, then cook for 5–6 minutes, until golden and cooked through.

Serve immediately with fresh fruit and a drizzle of maple syrup or honey.

For sweet potato waffles with crispy bacon & avocado, make the waffles as above. Meanwhile, cook 4 slices of bacon under a hot broiler until crispy. Halve an avocado, remove the pit and skin, then cut into thin slices. Arrange the avocado slices on top of the waffles and top with the crispy bacon.

squash & oat breakfast muffins

Makes **10**
Preparation time **10 minutes**
Cooking time **20–25 minutes**

large chunk of peeled
  butternut squash or **other
  squash** from the nonbulbous
  end (about 10 oz)
1²⁄₃ cups **whole-wheat flour**
1 tablespoon **baking powder**
1 ¹⁄₃ cups **rolled oats**
¹⁄₂ teaspoon **ground ginger**
¹⁄₂ teaspoon **ground
  cinnamon**
2 **eggs**
³⁄₄ cup **buttermilk**
¹⁄₄ cup **maple syrup** or **honey**
3 tablespoons **coconut** or
  sunflower oil
2 tablespoons **pumpkin
  seeds**

Line a muffin pan with 10 paper muffin liners.

Using a spiralizer fitted with a ¹⁄₈ inch spaghetti blade,
spiralize the squash. Coarsely snip any long spirals into
shorter lengths with a pair of scissors.

Sift together the flour and baking powder into a large
bowl. Stir in the oats and spices and mix well. In a separate
bowl, beat together the eggs, buttermilk, maple syrup or
honey, and oil. Pour over the dry ingredients and stir until
just combined, then stir in the spiralized squash.

Divide the batter among the muffin liners, then sprinkle
the tops with the pumpkin seeds. Bake in a preheated
oven, at 375°F, for 20–25 minutes, until risen and firm.

For chorizo & squash muffins, put 3¹⁄₂ oz diced
chorizo into a skillet and cook over high heat, until it is
crispy and has released its oil. Drain on paper towels.
Prepare the butternut squash as above. Sift together
2¹⁄₄ cups all-purpose flour and 1 tablespoon baking
powder in a large bowl. Stir in 1 cup shredded sharp
cheddar cheese. In a small bowl, whisk together 2 eggs,
³⁄₄ cup milk, and 6 tablespoons butter, melted. Pour over
the dry ingredients until just combined, then stir in the
spiralized squash and chorizo. Divide the batter among
the muffin liners and bake as above.

mini bacon, tomato & ricotta frittatas

Makes **6**
Preparation time **10 minutes**
Cooking time **20 minutes**

1 teaspoon **olive oil**, plus extra
  for greasing
3 **smoked bacon slices**, rind
  removed and chopped
1 **zucchini**, ends trimmed and
  halved widthwise
6 **eggs**
1 tablespoon chopped **chives**
¼ cup **ricotta cheese**
6 **cherry** or **baby plum**
  tomatoes, halved
salt and **black pepper**

Lightly oil 6 cups of a nonstick muffin top pan, each about 4 inches in diameter.

Heat the oil in a skillet over medium heat. Add the bacon and cook for 3–4 minutes, until lightly browned. Drain on paper towels.

Meanwhile, using a spiralizer fitted with a ⅛ inch spaghetti blade, spiralize the zucchini. Place the spiralized zucchini on a clean dish towel or paper towels and gently squeeze out any excess liquid. Coarsely snip any really long spirals in half with a pair of scissors.

Beat together the eggs and chives in a large bowl and season with salt and pepper. Add the spiralized zucchini and the bacon and stir well.

Divide the batter among the prepared pans, dot each with the ricotta, and add 2 tomato halves to each pan. Bake in a preheated oven, at 350°F, for 15 minutes, until set. Serve the frittatas warm. Any leftovers can be stored for up to 2–3 days in an airtight container in the refrigerator.

For mini sausage, bacon & tomato frittatas, broil 2 sausages until cooked through, then chop into small pieces. Make the frittatas as above, adding the sausages and ¼ cup shredded cheddar cheese to the egg mixture with the spiralized zucchini and bacon. Replace the ricotta with another ¼ cup shredded cheddar cheese. Bake as above.

easy pan-fried potato cakes

Serves **2**

Preparation time **5 minutes**

Cooking time **6–8 minutes**

1 large **russet potato** (about 8 oz), peeled and ends trimmed

⅓ cup **all-purpose flour**, plus extra for dusting

¼ teaspoon **baking powder**

2 tablespoons **unsalted butter**, melted, plus extra for greasing

salt and **black pepper**

Using a spiralizer fitted with a ⅛ inch spaghetti blade, spiralize the potato. Place the spiralized potato in a food processor and pulse until it resembles rice.

Put the flour, baking powder, and salt and pepper in a bowl, add the potato rice and butter, and combine gently with a spoon or your hands to make a dough.

Gently shape the dough into 2 balls using lightly floured hands, then transfer to a lightly floured surface. Roll out each ball into a circle about ¼ inch thick and prick all over with a fork.

Heat a skillet over medium heat. When hot, carefully smear with a little butter, add the potato cakes, and cook for 3–4 minutes on each side, until golden brown. Serve immediately with the topping of your choice.

For Scandi-style potato cakes, prepare the potato cakes as above, adding 2 tablespoons chopped chives to the batter. Mix together 2 tablespoons crème fraîche or sour cream, 1 teaspoon Dijon mustard, and 1 tablespoon freshly chopped dill in a small bowl and season to taste. Place a potato cake on each plate, then top each potato cake with spoonfuls of the crème fraîche mixture and a slice of smoked salmon. Serve with a wedge of lemon.

sausage & egg breakfast traybake

Serves **2**
Preparation time **5 minutes**
Cooking time **25 minutes**

2 large **potatoes**, skins
    scrubbed, ends trimmed and
    halved widthways
1 tablespoon **olive oil**
4 **pork sausages**
6 mini **portabellini**
    mushrooms
2 **smoked back bacon**
    rashers
2 **tomatoes**, halved
2 large **eggs**
salt and **black pepper**
tomato or **brown sauce**,
    to serve

Using a spiralizer fitted with a 6 mm (¼ inch) flat noodle blade, spiralize the potatoes.

Place the spiralized potatoes in a large bowl, add 2 teaspoons of the oil, season with salt and pepper, and toss well to coat in the oil and seasoning. Spread out the potatoes in a large, shallow nonstick roasting tin.

Bake in a preheated oven, 200°C (400°F), Gas Mark 6, for 5 minutes, then add the sausages and mushrooms and drizzle the remaining oil over the mushrooms. Return to the oven and bake for a further 10 minutes, turning the sausages and potatoes halfway through the cooking time. Add the bacon and tomatoes to the tin and bake for a further 5 minutes, or until the potatoes are crispy and sausages cooked through. Using the back of a spoon, make 2 holes in the potatoes. Crack an egg into each and season with salt and pepper. Return to the oven and bake for 3–4 minutes, until the eggs are softly set.

Carefully divide the mixture between 2 plates and serve immediately with tomato or brown sauce.

For a tomato & chilli jam to serve as an accompaniment, place 250 g (8 oz) roughly chopped tomatoes, 1 teaspoon grated root ginger, 1 coarsely chopped red chilli and 1 chopped garlic clove in a food processor and blend until fairly smooth. Pour into a saucepan and add 125 g (4 oz) soft light brown sugar, 50 ml (2 fl oz) red wine vinegar and a pinch of salt. Bring to the boil, stirring until the sugar has dissolved, then simmer for 20–25 minutes, until glossy and jammy.

corn & zucchini cakes

Serves **2**
Preparation time **5 minutes**
Cooking time **6–10 minutes**

1 **corn on the cob**
1 **zucchini**, ends trimmed and halved widthwise
4 **scallions**, thinly sliced
3 tablespoons **self-rising flour**
2 **eggs**, beaten
1 tablespoon **sunflower oil**, for frying
salt and **black pepper**

For the smashed avocado
1 large ripe **avocado**
juice of ½ **lime**
2 tablespoons chopped **fresh cilantro**
½ **red chili,** seeded and finely chopped

Hold the corn upright on a cutting board and, using a large sharp knife, carefully slice the kernels off the cob. Heat a griddle pan or skillet over high heat. Add the corn and cook for 2–3 minutes, until blackened slightly, then transfer to a large bowl.

Using a spiralizer fitted with a ⅛ inch spaghetti blade, spiralize the zucchini. Coarsely snip any really long spirals in half with a pair of scissors.

Add the spiralized zucchini to the corn with the scallions, flour, and eggs. Season with salt and plenty of pepper, then mix well.

Heat a little oil in a large nonstick skillet over medium heat. Add large spoonfuls of the batter, making 4 cakes, and cook for 2–3 minutes on each side, until lightly browned and cooked through.

Meanwhile, halve, pit, peel, and coarsely chop the avocado. Put into a bowl with the lime juice, cilantro, and chili and smash together with a fork to coarsely combine. Season to taste.

Place 2 cakes on each plate and serve immediately, topped with the smashed avocado.

For corn & zucchini cakes with poached eggs & sriracha sauce, make the cakes as above. Meanwhile, poach 2 eggs in a saucepan of simmering water for 3–4 minutes, until cooked and the yolks are runny. Remove the poached eggs with a slotted spoon. Serve the cakes topped with a poached egg and a drizzle of sriracha sauce.

kedgeree

Serves **2**
Preparation time **10 minutes**
Cooking time **10–12 minutes**

1 large **sweet potato**
   (about 10 oz), peeled,
   ends trimmed, and halved
   widthwise
1 small **onion**, ends trimmed
2 teaspoons **sunflower oil**
1 tablespoon **butter**
1 tablespoon **mild** or **medium
   curry paste**
7 oz boneless, skinless **cod**,
   cut into small chunks
½ cup **frozen peas**
juice of ½ **lemon**
2 **eggs**
2 tablespoons chopped **flat
   leaf parsley**
salt and **black pepper**
lemon wedges, to serve

Using a spiralizer fitted with a ⅛ inch spaghetti blade, spiralize the sweet potato.

Put the spiralized sweet potato into a food processor and pulse until it resembles rice.

Spiralize the onion and snip the spirals into 2–2½ inch lengths with a pair of scissors.

Heat the oil and butter in a large, nonstick skillet or wok with a lid over medium heat. Add the spiralized onion and cook for 2–3 minutes, until softened. Stir in the sweet potato rice and curry paste and cook for another 2 minutes, stirring to coat the rice in the paste. Stir in the cod, peas, and lemon juice, cover, and cook over low heat for 5–6 minutes, until the fish is cooked through and the sweet potato rice is tender.

Meanwhile, bring a small saucepan of water to a boil, add the eggs, and cook for 4 minutes. Drain, let cool slightly, and then shell the eggs.

Stir the parsley into the kedgeree and season to taste with salt and pepper. Cut the eggs into quarters.

Divide the kedgeree between 2 plates and top with the eggs. Serve with lemon wedges to squeeze over.

For cooling yogurt sauce, to serve as an accompaniment, mix together ¾ cup Greek yogurt with 1 tablespoon lemon juice and 2 tablespoons freshly chopped mint in a bowl.

zoodle egg rolls

Serves **2**
Preparation time **5 minutes**
Cooking time **8–10 minutes**

1 **zucchini**, ends trimmed and
   halved widthwise
3 **eggs**
cooking spray oil or a little
   sunflower oil, for frying
1 ripe **avocado**
4 slices **smoked salmon** or
   trout, cut into strips
salt and **black pepper**

Using a spiralizer fitted with a ⅛ inch spaghetti blade, spiralize the zucchini. Coarsely snip any extra-long spirals in half with a pair of scissors. Place the spiralized zucchini on a clean dish towel or paper towels and gently squeeze out any excess liquid.

Lightly beat together the eggs with salt and pepper in a small bowl. Heat a small, nonstick skillet over medium heat and spray or brush with oil. Add half the spiralized zucchini and stir-fry for 1 minute, then pour over half the eggs and swirl the pan to coat the bottom. Cook for 2–3 minutes, until the bottom is set, then flip over the omelet and cook for another 1 minute or until set.

Meanwhile, halve, pit, and peel the avocado and cut the flesh into strips.

Slide the omelet onto a board, add half the smoked salmon or trout and avocado, and roll up. Serve immediately. Repeat with the remaining ingredients to make 2 egg rolls.

For Indian egg rolls with smoked mackerel, make the egg rolls as above, whisking 2 teaspoons mild curry powder into the egg mixture and omitting the avocado and smoked salmon or trout. Meanwhile, mix together ¼ cup yogurt with 1 tablespoon mango chutney in a small bowl. Spread half the yogurt mixture over each omelet, divide 4 oz flaked, smoked mackerel between them, and roll up.

light bites

vegetable noodle miso soup

Serves **4**
Preparation time **5 minutes**
Cooking time **10 minutes**

3¾ cups hot **vegetable broth**
2 tablespoons **white miso paste**
2 teaspoons grated **fresh ginger**
2 **carrots**, peeled, ends trimmed, and halved widthwise
2 **zucchini**, ends trimmed and halved widthwise
1 cup fresh or frozen **edamame (soybeans)**
2 tablespoons chopped **fresh cilantro**

Put the vegetable broth, miso paste, and ginger into a saucepan. Bring to a boil, then reduce the heat and simmer for 3–4 minutes.

Meanwhile, using a spiralizer fitted with a ⅛ inch spaghetti blade, spiralize the carrots and zucchini.

Add the spiralized carrots and zucchini and the edamame to the soup and simmer for 3–4 minutes, until just tender. Stir in the cilantro and serve immediately.

For chicken & corn noodle soup, spiralize the vegetables as above. Put 3¾ cups chicken broth into a saucepan with 1 teaspoon dark soy sauce and 2 chopped scallions and bring to a boil. Add the spiralized carrots and zucchini, 1 cup canned or frozen corn kernels, and ⅔ cup cooked shredded chicken. Simmer for 3–4 minutes, then ladle the soup into bowls and sprinkle with a few extra chopped scallions.

autumnal minestrone soup

Serves **4**
Preparation time **15 minutes**
Cooking time **15 minutes**

1 **onion**, ends trimmed
½ small **celeriac (celery root)**,
   peeled and cut into 5 inch
   chunks
2 **carrots**, peeled, ends
   trimmed, and halved
   widthwise
1 **zucchini**, ends trimmed and
   halved widthwise
1 tablespoon **olive oil**
1 **garlic clove**, crushed
3 oz **pancetta**, cubed
1 (14½ oz) can **diced
   tomatoes**
3 cups hot **vegetable broth**
⅓ head of **savoy cabbage**,
   thinly sliced
1½ cups cooked **cranberry
   beans**
salt and **black pepper**

To serve
freshly grated **Parmesan
   cheese**
basil leaves
crusty bread

Using a spiralizer fitted with a ⅛ inch spaghetti blade, spiralize the onion, celeriac, carrots, and zucchini, keeping them separate.

Heat the oil in a large saucepan. Add the spiralized onion and celeriac and the garlic and pancetta, then cook over low heat for 3–4 minutes, until the onion is soft but not browned. Add the spiralized carrots, tomatoes, broth, cabbage, and beans, then cover and simmer for 5 minutes or until the celeriac is just tender. Stir in the spiralized zucchini, cover, and cook for another 3–4 minutes, until all the vegetables are tender. Season the soup to taste.

Ladle the soup into 4 bowls, sprinkle with the Parmesan and basil leaves, and serve with chunks of crusty bread.

For summer minestrone soup, spiralize 1 onion and 2 zucchini as above. Heat 1 tablespoon olive oil in a large saucepan and cook the onion and 1 crushed garlic clove for 3–4 minutes, until softened but not browned. Stir in 4 cups vegetable broth and bring to a boil. Add 8 oz asparagus tips, ⅔ cup fresh or frozen peas, and 1⅓ cups double-shelled fava beans. Cover and simmer for 3–4 minutes, then add the spiralized zucchini, cover, and cook for another 2 minutes or until the vegetables are tender. Stir in 3 tablespoons pesto sauce and season to taste.

vietnamese chicken pho

Serves **2**
Preparation time **10 minutes**
Cooking time **25 minutes**

2 teaspoons **sunflower oil**
1 teaspoon **black peppercorns**
1 **lemon grass stalk**, trimmed
and sliced
½ **cinnamon stick**
1 **star anise**
1 inch piece **fresh ginger**,
peeled and thinly sliced
2½ cups hot **chicken broth**
1⅔ cups **boiling water**
1 boneless, skinless **chicken
breast**
¾ **daikon**, peeled, ends
trimmed, and halved
widthwise
½ **carrot**, peeled and ends
trimmed
2 teaspoons **Thai fish sauce**
juice of 1 **lime**
3 **scallions**, thinly shredded
½ fat **red chili,** seeded and
thinly sliced
a handful of **cilantro leaves**
2 **lime wedges**, to serve

Heat the oil in a large saucepan, add the peppercorns, lemon grass, cinnamon, star anise, and ginger, and cook for 1–2 minutes to release their aromas. Add the broth, measured water, and chicken breast. Bring to a boil, then cover and simmer for 20 minutes or until the chicken is cooked through.

Meanwhile, using a spiralizer fitted with a ⅛ inch spaghetti blade, spiralize the daikon and carrot, keeping them separate.

Remove the chicken from the broth and set aside. Strain the broth through a strainer into a small bowl and return to the pan. Shred the chicken using 2 forks, then add to the broth. Stir in the fish sauce, lime juice, spiralized daikon, and the scallions and cook for 3 minutes or until the noodles are tender.

Divide the pho between 2 bowls and sprinkle with the chili, spiralized carrot, and the cilantro. Serve immediately with lime wedges to squeeze over the top.

For vietnamese chicken salad, spiralize the daikon, 1 carrot, and ½ cucumber, using the spaghetti blade, and put into a large bowl. Add 1 cup cooked shredded chicken, ¾ cup bean sprouts, and 2 tablespoons each of freshly chopped mint and cilantro. In a small bowl, whisk together 1 tablespoon rice wine vinegar, 2 tablespoons sweet chili sauce, 2 teaspoons Thai fish sauce, and 2 tablespoons lime juice. Pour the dressing over the salad and toss gently. Divide between 2 bowls and sprinkle with a handful of chopped roasted peanuts.

winter vegetable & red lentil soup

Serves **2–3**
Preparation time **10 minutes**
Cooking time **25 minutes**

1 **onion**, ends trimmed
1 **sweet potato**, peeled,
    ends trimmed, and halved
    widthwise
1 **carrot**, peeled, ends
    trimmed, and halved
    widthwise
1 **parsnip**, peeled, ends
    trimmed, and halved
    widthwise
1 tablespoon **sunflower oil**
1 **red chili,** seeded and
    chopped
1 tablespoon **ground cumin**
¼ cup **red lentils**, rinsed in
    cold water and drained
3 cups hot **vegetable broth**
salt and **black pepper**

To serve
Greek yogurt
chopped **fresh cilantro**

Using a spiralizer fitted with a ⅛ inch spaghetti blade, spiralize the onion, sweet potato, carrot, and parsnip, keeping the onion separate.

Heat the oil in a saucepan, add the spiralized onion, and cook over low heat for 3–4 minutes, until softened. Stir in the chili and cumin and cook for 1 minute, then stir in the lentils.

Add the broth and bring to a boil, then reduce the heat, cover, and simmer for 15 minutes, stirring occasionally, until the lentils are tender. Add all the remaining spiralized vegetables and simmer for another 4–5 minutes, until the soup has thickened and the vegetables are tender. Season to taste.

Ladle the soup into bowls and serve with a dollop of yogurt and the cilantro.

For winter vegetable & pasta soup, prepare the spiralized vegetables as above. Heat 1 tablespoon olive oil in a saucepan and add the spiralized onion and 1 crushed garlic clove. Cook over low heat for 3–4 minutes, until softened. Add 2½ cups hot vegetable broth and 1 cup tomato puree or sauce, bring to a boil, then add 2 oz small pasta shapes or broken spaghetti. Cover and simmer for 5–6 minutes, then add the remaining spiralized vegetables. Simmer for another 4–5 minutes, until the vegetables and pasta are tender. Ladle the soup into 2 bowls and serve with freshly grated Parmesan cheese.

zucchini, feta & mint fritters

Serves **4**
Preparation time **10 minutes**
Cooking time **15 minutes**

3 **zucchini**, ends trimmed and
    cut in half widthwise
4 **scallions**, chopped
¼ cup chopped **mint**
1 cup **all-purpose flour**
1 teaspoon **baking powder**
1 teaspoon **ground cumin**
2 **eggs**, lightly beaten
¾ cup crumbled **feta cheese**
1 tablespoon **olive oil**, for
    frying
salt and **black pepper**
tomato salsa, to serve

Using a spiralizer fitted with a ⅛ inch spaghetti blade, spiralize the zucchini.

Mix together the spiralized zucchini, scallions, mint, flour, baking powder, and cumin in a large bowl. Stir in the eggs, mix well, and season with salt and pepper. Gently fold in the feta.

Heat a little oil in a large skillet over medium heat. Cooking 4 fritters at a time, add heaping tablespoons of the batter to the pan, flatten slightly, and cook for 3 minutes on each side, or until golden. Repeat until all the batter is used. Serve the fritters with a spoonful of tomato salsa.

For zucchini & corn fritters prepare the zucchini as above. Mix together the spiralized zucchini, 1 cup fresh or frozen corn kernels, 4 chopped scallions, 1 seeded and finely chopped red chili, 1 cup all-purpose flour, 1 teaspoon baking powder, 2 lightly beaten eggs, and ¼ cup freshly chopped cilantro in a large bowl. Season with a little salt and black pepper. Cook as above and serve with lime wedges and guacamole.

spicy carrot & cilantro fritters

Makes **about 6**
Preparation time **10 minutes**
Cooking time **15 minutes**

3 large **carrots**, peeled,
   ends trimmed, and halved
   widthwise
1 small **onion**, ends trimmed
½ cup **chickpea (besan) flour**
1 teaspoon **baking powder**
1 teaspoon **ground cumin**
1 teaspoon **garam masala**
½ teaspoon **ground turmeric**
½ teaspoon **salt**
2 **eggs**, lightly beaten
scant ½ cup **buttermilk** or
   plain yogurt
1 **garlic clove**, crushed
2 tablespoons chopped **fresh
   cilantro**
1 tablespoon **olive** or
   sunflower oil, for frying

To serve
cucumber dip
lemon wedges

Using a spiralizer fitted with a ⅛ inch spaghetti blade, spiralize the carrots and onion.

Mix together the flour, baking powder, spices, and salt in a large bowl. Stir in the eggs and buttermilk or yogurt to make a smooth batter. Add the spiralized vegetables, the garlic, and cilantro and mix until combined.

Heat a little of the oil in a large nonstick skillet over medium heat. Cooking 4 fritters at a time, add heaping tablespoons of the batter to the pan, flatten slightly, and cook for 3 minutes on each side, until golden. Repeat until all the batter is used. Serve the fritters with a cucumber dip and lemon wedges to squeeze over them.

For cilantro & yogurt sauce to serve as an accompaniment, put ¾ cup Greek yogurt into a food processor with 1 crushed garlic clove, 2 teaspoons lemon juice, and ½ cup chopped fresh cilantro. Process until you have a bright green sauce. Season to taste and serve with the fritters.

cauli-crust mediterranean pizza

Serves **2**
Preparation time **10 minutes**
Cooking time **20–25 minutes**

For the crust
4 cups **cauliflower florets**
1 teaspoon **dried oregano**
½ teaspoon **garlic salt**
⅓ cup grated **Parmesan cheese**
1 **egg**, beaten
salt and **black pepper**

For the topping
½ **zucchini**, ends trimmed
2 tablespoons **tomato paste**
¼ cup shredded **mozzarella cheese**
½ **yellow bell pepper**, cored, seeded, and diced
6 **cherry tomatoes**, halved
3 oz **soft goat cheese**, coarsely chopped
basil leaves

Put a large nonstick baking sheet into a preheated oven, at 400°F.

Put the cauliflower into a food processor and pulse until it resembles rice. Transfer to a microwavable bowl, cover with plastic wrap, and pierce the top, then cook on full power in a microwave for 4 minutes or until tender. Let cool slightly, then place in a clean dish towel and squeeze over a sink to remove the excess liquid. Return to the bowl and add the oregano, garlic salt, Parmesan, egg, and salt and pepper, and mix well.

Transfer the mixture to a piece of nonstick parchment paper. Using your hands, flatten into a thin circle, about 9 inch in diameter, then transfer to the hot baking sheet. Bake for 12–15 minutes, until golden brown.

Meanwhile, using a spiralizer fitted with a ribbon blade, spiralize the zucchini.

Spread the tomato paste over the crust and sprinkle with the mozzarella. Top with the spiralized zucchini, yellow bell pepper, and tomatoes, then dot over the goat cheese.

Return the pizza to the oven and bake for 5–7 minutes, until the vegetables are cooked through and the cheese is melted. Sprinkle with the basil and serve.

For cauli-crust pepperoni pizza, prepare and bake the crust as above. Spread 2–3 tablespoons prepared pizza sauce over the crust, then sprinkle with ¼ cup shredded mozzarella cheese, top with 10 slices pepperoni, and arrange the spiralized zucchini and the cherry tomatoes over the top. Sprinkle with another ¼ cup shredded mozzarella cheese and bake as above.

mexican baked potato nests

Serves **4**

Preparation time **10 minutes**

Cooking time **20 minutes**

2 medium-large **russet
   potatoes** (about 12 oz),
   peeled and ends trimmed

1 small **onion**, ends trimmed

2 tablespoons **olive oil**

3 oz **chorizo**, diced

1 **garlic clove**, crushed

1 mild **green chili,** seeded and
   finely chopped

½ small **yellow bell pepper**,
   cored, seeded, and diced

¾ cup canned **diced
   tomatoes**

1 teaspoon **ketchu**p

1 tablespoon chopped **fresh
   cilantro**

4 **eggs**

smoked paprika, for
   sprinkling

salt and **black pepper**

Using a spiralizer fitted with a ⅛ inch spaghetti blade,
spiralize the potatoes and onion.

Put the spiralized potatoes into a large bowl, add the oil,
season with salt and pepper, then toss the potatoes to
coat them in the oil and seasoning. Divide the potatoes
among 4 holes in a muffin top pan, each about 4 inches
in diameter. Bake in a preheated oven, at 350°F, for
10 minutes.

Put the chorizo into a skillet and cook over medium heat
for 2–3 minutes, until the oil has been released. Add
the onion, garlic, chili, and bell pepper and cook, stirring
frequently, for 2–3 minutes, until the bell pepper is soft.
Stir in the tomatoes and ketchup and season with salt and
pepper. Bring to a boil, then reduce the heat and simmer
for 2–3 minutes, until the mixture has thickened. Stir in
the cilantro and season to taste.

Remove the potato nests from the oven and use a
spoon to press down the center of each nest to make a
hollow. Divide the tomato mixture among the nests and
then use a spoon to make 4 shallow wells.

Break an egg into each shallow well. Return to the oven
and bake for another 6–7 minutes, until the eggs are
just set. Sprinkle with a little smoked paprika and serve.

crispy onion bhajis

Makes **about 12**
Preparation time **10 minutes**
Cooking time **10 minutes**

2 **onions**, ends trimmed
1 cup **chickpea (besan) flour**
½ teaspoon **baking powder**
1 **green chili,** finely chopped
2 tablespoons chopped **fresh cilantro**
1 teaspoon **salt**
1 teaspoon **ground cumin**
½ teaspoon **ground turmeric**
1 tablespoon **sunflower oil**
1 teaspoon **lemon juice**
5–6 tablespoons **water**
4 cups **vegetable** or **sunflower oil**, for deep frying

Cucumber & Mint Raita (see page 168), to serve

Using a spiralizer fitted with a ¼ inch flat noodle blade, spiralize the onions.

Put the flour, baking powder, chili, cilantro, salt, cumin, and turmeric into a large bowl and mix well. Stir in the sunflower oil, lemon juice, and measured water to make a thick batter. Add the spiralized onions and stir to coat with the batter.

Heat the vegetable or sunflower oil in a wok or deep, heavy saucepan to 350–375°F, or until a cube of bread dropped into the oil turns golden brown in 30 seconds. Alternatively, you can use a deep fryer.

Carefully drop tablespoonfuls of the batter into the hot oil, cooking 4 bhajis at a time, and deep-fry for 2–3 minutes, until golden. Remove from the oil with a slotted spoon, drain on paper towels, and keep warm while you cook the remaining bhaji mixture. Serve the bhajis hot with cucumber and mint raita.

For sweet potato bhajis, make the onion bhajis as above, replacing the 2 onions with 1 small red onion and 1 sweet potato, and spiralizing both the onion and sweet potato. Serve with mango chutney.

marmite & cheese potato strings

Serves **4 as a snack**
Preparation time **5 minutes**
Cooking time **20–22 minutes**

2 **russet potatoes**, skins
   scrubbed and ends trimmed
1 tablespoon **sunflower oil**
1 tablespoon **Marmite** or
   yeast extract
¼ cup shredded **sharp**
   cheddar cheese
black pepper

Line a large baking sheet with nonstick parchment paper.

Using a spiralizer fitted with a ⅛ inch spaghetti blade, spiralize the potatoes. Coarsely snip the spirals into 5–6 inch lengths with a pair of scissors.

Put the spiralized potatoes into a large bowl, add 2 teaspoons of the oil, and season with a little pepper. Toss the strings to coat in the oil and seasoning.

Spread out the spiralized potatoes in a single layer on the prepared baking sheet and bake in a preheated oven, at 400°F, for 10 minutes.

Meanwhile, in a large bowl, mix together the Marmite or yeast extract, remaining oil, and the cheese.

Remove the strings from the oven and toss in the Marmite mixture, stirring until evenly coated. Return to the oven and bake for another 10–12 minutes, until crispy, turning once. (Remove any strings that are already cooked when you turn over the potatoes.) Remove from the oven and let cool. The strings can be stored for up to 2–3 days in an airtight container.

For tomato & cheese potato strings, prepare and bake the potatoes for the first 10 minutes, as above. Meanwhile, mix together 2 tablespoons tomato paste and ⅓ cup finely grated Parmesan cheese in a bowl. Remove the strings from the oven and toss in the tomato mixture, stirring until evenly coated. Return to the oven and bake for another 10–12 minutes as above.

kohlrabi carpaccio with prosciutto

Serves **2 as an appetizer**
Preparation time **5 minutes,
plus marinating**

1 small **kohlrabi**, peeled and
ends trimmed
½ **lemon**
2 teaspoons **olive oil**
a few small **lemon thyme
sprigs**
1 oz piece **Parmesan cheese**
4 slices **prosciutto**
sea salt and **black pepper**

Using a spiralizer fitted with a ribbon blade, spiralize
the kohlrabi.

Arrange the spiralized kohlrabi on a large plate, then
squeeze the lemon juice over it and drizzle with the oil.
Sprinkle with a little sea salt, pepper, and thyme, then let
marinate for about 1 hour.

When you are ready to serve, divide the kohlrabi
carpaccio between 2 plates. Using a vegetable peeler,
shave the Parmesan over the kohlrabi, then arrange the
ham over the top and serve immediately.

For fennel carpaccio with bresaola, trim the ends
and leafy tops from 1 large fennel bulb, reserving the
feathery fronds. Spiralize the fennel using a ribbon
blade. Arrange the spiralized fennel on a large plate.
Whisk together the juice of ½ lemon and 2 teaspoons
olive oil in a bowl and season with salt and black pepper.
Coarsely chop the reserved fronds and add to the
dressing. Pour the dressing over the fennel, then top
with 16 slices of bresaola, a handful of arugula leaves,
and Parmesan shavings.

spicy crab & papaya lettuce wraps

Serves **4**

Preparation time **15 minutes, plus marinating**

1 small **green papaya**, about 450 g (14½ oz), peeled and ends trimmed
1 **carrot**, peeled, ends trimmed and halved widthways
4 **spring onions**, finely sliced
200 g (7 oz) **white crab meat**
2 tablespoons chopped **fresh coriander**
12 large **Little Gem leaves**

For the dressing
1 **passion fruit**
juice of 1 **lime**
1 teaspoon **palm** or **soft brown sugar**
2 teaspoons finely grated **fresh root ginger**
1 teaspoon **fish sauce**
½–1 **red chilli**, deseeded and finely chopped

Cut the papaya in half widthways and tap out the seeds. Attach the narrow end of one half of the papaya to a spiralizer fitted with a 3 mm (⅛ inch) spaghetti blade and spiralize. Repeat with the remaining papaya half. Place the spiralized papaya in a large bowl. Spiralize the carrot and add to the bowl with the spring onions.

To make the dressing, halve the passion fruit and, using a teaspoon, scoop out the pulp into a small bowl. Add all the remaining dressing ingredients, adding the chilli to taste, and stir until the sugar has dissolved.

Add the crab to the papaya mixture and pour over half the dressing. Toss well and leave to marinate for about 10 minutes, stirring halfway through the marinating time. Stir in the coriander.

Place the lettuce leaves on a large plate and spoon in the papaya and crab mixture. Serve immediately with the remaining dressing in a small bowl to spoon over.

For papaya & prawn summer rolls, prepare 1 green papaya and 1 carrot as above, and place in a bowl with 50 g (2 oz) bean sprouts, 4 tablespoons chopped fresh coriander and 250 g (8 oz) peeled cooked prawns. Squeeze over the juice of ½ lime and stir well. Take 8 rice paper wraps, and place them, one at a time, in a bowl of warm water, for 30 seconds, until softened and opaque. Remove and shake off excess water. Place a wrapper on a chopping board, brush with a little fish sauce, add 2 mint leaves, then place some of the prawn and vegetable mixture down the centre. Fold over both ends of the wrap, then roll up. Cover with a damp cloth. Repeat with the remaining wrappers. Serve with sweet chilli sauce.

greek salad pita pockets

Serves **4**

Preparation time **10 minutes**

1 small **red onion**, ends
   trimmed

5 inch piece **cucumber**, ends
   trimmed and cut in half
   widthwise

8 **cherry tomatoes**, quartered

6 **pitted black olives**,
   chopped

¾ cup crumbled **feta cheese**

1 tablespoon **lemon juice**

2 tablespoons **extra virgin
   olive oil**

1 teaspoon **dried oregano**

4 **pita breads**

1 **Little Gem lettuce**,
   shredded

salt and **black pepper**

Using a spiralizer fitted with a ⅛ inch spaghetti blade, spiralize the onion and cucumber.

Put the spiralized onion and cucumber into a large bowl with the tomatoes, olives, and feta.

Whisk together the lemon juice, oil, and oregano in a small bowl, then season to taste with salt and pepper. Pour the dressing over the salad ingredients and gently toss together.

Lightly toast the pita breads under a preheated medium-hot broiler for about 1 minute on each side.

Slice each pita bread in half horizontally. Fill the pita pockets with a little lettuce and top with the feta mixture. Serve immediately.

For Greek salad with crispy pita chips, make the salad and dressing as above. Open the pita bread to make 8 halves, then cut into bite-size strips. Put the pita strips onto a baking sheet, brush both sides with a little oil, and season with salt. Bake in a preheated oven, at 350°F, for 8–10 minutes, until crisp and golden, turning halfway through the cooking time. Divide the salad among 4 plates and top with the crispy pita chips.

mini sweet potato & ricotta frittatas

Makes **8**
Preparation time **5 minutes**
Cooking time **25 minutes**

1 large **sweet potato** (about
  8 oz), peeled, ends trimmed,
  and halved widthwise
1 small **onion**, ends trimmed
1 tablespoon **olive oil**, plus a
  little extra for oiling
2 cups **baby spinach**
6 **eggs**
2 tablespoons chopped **sage**
1 tablespoon chopped **chives**
1 teaspoon **paprika**
4 oz **ricotta cheese**, broken
  into small chunks
salt and **black pepper**
crisp green salad, to serve

Lightly oil 8 cups of a nonstick muffin pan. Using a
spiralizer fitted with a ⅛ inch spaghetti blade, spiralize
the sweet potato and onion.

Heat the oil in a large skillet over medium heat, add
the spiralized sweet potato and onion, and cook for
3 minutes or until the sweet potato has softened slightly.
Add the spinach and cook for another 1 minute or until
the spinach has wilted. Let the sweet potato mixture
cool slightly.

Beat the eggs in a large bowl with the herbs and
paprika, then season with salt and pepper. Add the
sweet potato mixture and mix well. Stir in the ricotta.

Divide the mixture among the cups in the prepared
muffin pan and bake in a preheated oven, at 350°F, for
20 minutes or until set. Serve the frittatas immediately
with a crisp green salad.

For sweet potato & blue cheese frittatas, make
the frittatas as above, replacing the ricotta cheese with
4 oz crumbled blue cheese, such as Stilton or dolcelatte.

salads

zucchini, tomato & mozzarella salad

Serves **4**

Preparation time **10 minutes, plus marinating**

2 **zucchini**, ends trimmed and halved widthwise

2 cups **cherry** or **baby plum tomatoes**, halved

¼ cup **pitted black olives**

1 (8 oz) ball **buffalo mozzarella cheese**, drained

3 tablespoons **pine nuts**, toasted

12 **basil leaves**

For the dressing

1 **garlic clove**, crushed

1 teaspoon **aged balsamic vinegar**

1 teaspoon **capers**, chopped

juice of 1 **lemon**

2 tablespoons **olive oil**

black pepper

Using a spiralizer fitted with a ribbon blade, spiralize the zucchini. Coarsely snip any extra-long ribbons in half with a pair of scissors.

Put the spiralized zucchini into a large bowl and add the tomatoes and olives.

Whisk together all the dressing ingredients in a small bowl to make the dressing. Pour the dressing over the salad, reserving a little, then let marinate for about 10 minutes.

Put the zucchini, tomatoes, and olives onto a platter. Tear the mozzarella into pieces and arrange over the salad, then sprinkle with the pine nuts and basil leaves. Drizzle with the remaining dressing and serve immediately.

For roasted tomatoes to replace the fresh tomatoes in the salad, put the halved cherry or baby plum tomatoes into a roasting pan and bake in a preheated oven, at 300°F, for 45 minutes, or until the tomatoes are slightly caramelized.

apple, fennel & gorgonzola salad

Serves **4**
Preparation time **10 minutes**

1 large **fennel bulb**, ends
  trimmed and leafy tops
  chopped
1 large **red eating apple**, ends
  trimmed
1 large **green eating apple**,
  ends trimmed
125 g (4 oz) **radishes**, thinly
  sliced
75 g (3 oz) **pea shoots**
50 g (2 oz) **walnut halves**
125 g (4 oz) **Gorgonzola
  cheese**, broken into small
  pieces

For the dressing
2 tablespoons **extra virgin
  olive oil**
2 tablespoons **cider vinegar**
2 teaspoons **wholegrain
  mustard**
2 teaspoons **honey**
salt and **black pepper**

First, make the dressing. In a small bowl, whisk together
all the dressing ingredients and season to taste with a
little salt and pepper.

Using a spiralizer fitted with a ribbon blade, spiralize
the fennel and apples. Snip any really long ribbons into
shorter lengths with scissors.

Place the spiralized fennel and apples in a bowl and
pour over half the dressing. Add the radishes and toss
gently to coat.

Divide the pea shoots between 4 plates or arrange
on a platter, then add the apple and fennel mixture.
Scatter over the walnuts, Gorgonzola and chopped
fennel tops. Drizzle over the remaining dressing and
serve immediately.

For apple, lentil & walnut salad, whisk together
2 tablespoons balsamic vinegar, 3 tablespoons walnut
oil, 1 teaspoon French mustard and a little salt and
black pepper in a small bowl. Place 125 g (4 oz) baby
spinach, 1 x 400 g (13 oz) can green lentils in water,
drained and rinsed, 125 g (4 oz) roasted chopped red
peppers in brine or oil, drained, and 50 g (2 oz) walnut
pieces in a bowl and pour over most of the dressing.
Toss well. Spiralize 2 apples as above and gently stir
into the salad. Divide between 4 plates and crumble
over 125 g (4 oz) goats' cheese. Serve immediately,
drizzled with the remaining dressing.

pear, ham & blue cheese salad

Serves **2**

Preparation time **5 minutes**

1 large or 2 small **red-skinned pears**, pointy ends trimmed

juice of 1 **lemon**

1 tablespoon **extra virgin olive oil**

3½ cups **arugula leaves**

4 slices **Serrano ham**

3 oz **Roquefort** or **dolcelatte cheese**, cubed

salt and **black pepper**

Using a spiralizer fitted with a ¼ inch flat noodle blade, spiralize the pears. Put the spiralized pears into a bowl and spoon over a little of the lemon juice to prevent them from turning brown.

Whisk together the remaining lemon juice and the oil in a small bowl and season with salt and pepper.

Divide the arugula leaves between 2 plates, top with the spiralized pears and ham, and sprinkle with the cheese. Drizzle with the dressing and serve immediately.

For pear, endive & Manchego salad with honey dressing, spiralize 1 large or 2 small pears as above, put into a bowl, and drizzle with 1 tablespoon lemon juice. Separate the leaves from 2 heads of endive and divide between 2 plates. Top with the spiralized pears and 2 tablespoons toasted hazelnuts. In a small bowl, whisk together 1 tablespoon honey, 1 teaspoon Dijon mustard, and 2 tablespoons extra virgin olive oil, then season to taste. Drizzle the dressing over the salad, then shred 1 oz Manchego cheese over the top. Serve immediately.

chicken with pistachio tabbouleh

Serves **2**

Preparation time **15 minutes,
plus marinating**

Cooking time **8–12 minutes**

2 teaspoons grated **unwaxed
orange zest**

¼ cup **orange juice**

2 tablespoons **olive oil**

2 tablespoons **pomegranate
molasses**

2 boneless, skinless **chicken
breasts**

2 **fresh beets**, scrubbed and
ends trimmed

¼ cup chopped **flat leaf
parsley**

¼ cup chopped **mint**

2 cups **baby kale** or **spinach**

½ cup **pomegranate seeds**

3 tablespoons **pistachios**

salt and **black pepper**

Mix together half of the orange zest, orange juice, oil, and pomegranate molasses in a large nonreactive bowl, add the chicken breasts, and let marinate for about 15 minutes.

Meanwhile, using a spiralizer fitted with a ⅛ inch spaghetti blade, spiralize the beets. Put the spiralized beets into a food processor and pulse until it resembles rice.

Transer the beet rice to a large bowl and stir in the herbs, kale or spinach, pomegranate seeds, and the pistachios.

Mix together the remaining orange zest, orange juice, oil, and pomegranate molasses in a separate small bowl. Season to taste with salt and pepper, then pour it over the beet tabbouleh and toss well.

Heat a ridged grill pan until hot. Add the chicken and cook over medium heat for 4–6 minutes on each side, basting occasionally, until cooked through.

Divide the tabbouleh between 2 bowls. Thinly slice the chicken, arrange over the top, and serve immediately.

For tahini sauce to serve as an accompaniment, whisk together 3 tablespoons tahini, 3 tablespoons plain yogurt, the juice of 1 large lemon, 2 crushed garlic cloves, and 2 tablespoons water in a bowl until smooth.

chicken, zucchini & quinoa salad

Serves **4**

Preparation time **10 minutes**

Cooking time **20–30 minutes**

1 cup **uncooked quinoa**, rinsed

2 **zucchini**, ends trimmed and halved widthwise

1 tablespoon **olive oil**

2 teaspoons **sumac**

3 boneless, skinless **chicken breasts**

finely grated zest and juice of 1 large **unwaxed lemon**

1 tablespoon **extra virgin olive oil**

¼ cup chopped **mint**

¾ cup **pistachios**, coarsely chopped

¾ cup **pomegranate seeds**

salt and **black pepper**

Put the quinoa into a saucepan, cover with 2½ cups cold water, and add a little salt. Bring to a boil, then reduce the heat and simmer for 10–15 minutes or until the quinoa is tender and has absorbed most of the water. Remove from the heat, cover, and let stand while you prepare the rest of the salad.

Using a spiralizer fitted with a ribbon blade, spiralize the zucchini.

Put the olive oil and sumac into shallow dish and season with salt and pepper. Add the chicken and toss to coat.

Heat a ridged grill pan until hot. Add the chicken and cook over medium heat for 4–6 minutes on each side or until cooked through. Transfer the chicken to a plate and set aside. Add the spiralized zucchini to the grill pan and cook for about 2 minutes or until lightly charred.

Put the quinoa into a large bowl and add the lemon zest and juice, extra virgin olive oil, mint, and pistachios, then mix well and season to taste. Gently stir in the zucchini and pomegranate seeds.

Thinly slice the chicken breasts. Divide the quinoa salad almong 4 plates, top with the chicken, and serve.

For lemony chicken, zucchini & mixed herb salad, cook the chicken as above. Spiralize 2 zucchini with a spaghetti blade, then pat dry and snip into small pieces. In a bowl, mix together ½ cup Greek yogurt, the finely grated zest and juice of 1 lemon, and ¼ cup each of chopped dill, flat leaf parsley, and mint. Season to taste. Add the zucchini and stir to coat. Divide among 4 plates and top with the thinly sliced chicken.

thai beef salad

Serves **4**
Preparation time **15 minutes**
Cooking time **10–15 minutes**

1 small **cucumber**, ends
   trimmed and halved
   widthwise
2 **carrots**, peeled, ends
   trimmed, and halved
   widthwise
1 **daikon**, peeled, ends
   trimmed, and halved
   widthwise
1 lb **tenderloin steak**
1 tablespoon **sunflower** or
   peanut oil
½ head of **napa cabbage** or
   iceberg lettuce, finely sliced
handful of **peanuts**, coarsely
   chopped (optional)
salt and **black pepper**

For the dressing
2 tablespoons packed **light
   brown sugar**
2 tablespoons **Thai fish sauce**
juice of 3 **limes**
3 **garlic cloves**, crushed
1 **Thai chili,** seeded and finely
   chopped
⅓ cup chopped **fresh cilantro**

First, make the dressing. Whisk together all the dressing ingredients in a small bowl until the sugar has dissolved.

Using a spiralizer fitted with a ⅛ inch spaghetti blade, spiralize the cucumber, carrots, and daikon.

Put the spiralized vegetables into a bowl and pour over half the dressing. Let the salad marinate while you cook the beef.

Brush the steak with the oil and season with salt and pepper. Heat a ridged grill pan until smoking hot, then add the steak and cook over medium-high heat for 3–6 minutes on each side or until cooked to your preference. Transfer the steak to a plate and let rest for 5 minutes, then thinly slice.

Stir the napa cabbage or lettuce into the salad just before you are ready to serve. Divide the salad among 4 plates or place on a large platter or board, top with the beef, and drizzle with the remaining dressing. Sprinkle with the peanuts, if using, and serve immediately.

For raw pad thai salad, spiralize 2 carrots, 1 daikon, and 2 zucchini as above. In a bowl, whisk together 3 tablespoons peanut butter, 3 tablespoons soy sauce, the juice of 1 lime, 1 tablespoon grated fresh ginger, 1 tablespoon packed light brown sugar, 1 tablespoon toasted sesame oil, and a pinch dried chili flakes. Put the vegetables into a bowl with 1 cup bean sprouts and ¼ cup chopped fresh cilantro, pour the dressing over the salad, and mix well.

jerusalem artichoke & bacon salad

Serves **4**
Preparation time **12 minutes**
Cooking time **10 minutes**

2 tablespoons **olive oil**
8 **smoked bacon slices**,
  chopped
1 **garlic clove**, crushed
12 oz large **Jerusalem
  artichokes**, scrubbed
2 tablespoons **flat leaf
  parsley**
2 tablespoons **balsamic
  vinegar**
1 tablespoon **lemon juice**
8 **Little Gem lettuce**,
  quartered
a small handful of **Parmesan
  cheese shavings**
salt and **black pepper**

Heat 1 tablespoon of the oil in a large skillet or wok over medium heat. Add the bacon and garlic and cook for 2–3 minutes, stirring occasionally, until the bacon is lightly browned.

Meanwhile, using a spiralizer fitted with a ribbon blade, spiralize the Jerusalem artichokes. Snip any extra-long ribbons in half with a pair of scissors.

Immediately add the spiralized artichokes to the bacon in the skillet (to prevent the artichokes from discoloring) and stir-fry for 3–4 minutes, until the bacon and artichokes start to turn crispy. Remove from the heat and stir in the parsley.

Whisk together the remaining oil, the vinegar, and lemon juice in a small bowl, and season with salt and pepper.

Divide the lettuce among 4 plates and top with the warm bacon and artichoke mixture. Spoon a little dressing over the mixture, sprinkle with Parmesan shavings, and serve immediately.

For crispy Parmesan croutons to serve with the salad, cut 3½ oz ciabatta (about ⅓ of an average-size loaf) into ¾ inch cubes. Put into a large bowl and toss with 2 tablespoons olive oil, 2 tablespoons freshly grated Parmesan cheese, the finely grated zest of ½ unwaxed lemon, and some black pepper. Transfer to a baking sheet and bake on the middle shelf of a preheated oven, at 400° F, for 8–10 minutes, until golden.

tuna with carrot & cucumber salad

Serves **2**

Preparation time **15 minutes,
plus marinating**

Cooking time **4–6 minutes**

2 **tuna steaks** (about 6 oz),
about **1** inch thick

½ **cucumber**, ends trimmed
and halved widthwise

1 **carrot**, peeled, ends
trimmed, and halved
widthwise

2 **Little Gem lettuce**, ends
trimmed and each cut into
quarters

4 **scallions**, thinly sliced

2 teaspoons **sesame seeds**,
toasted

For the marinade

finely grated zest and juice of
2 **unwaxed limes**

¼ cup **soy sauce**

1 **garlic clove**, crushed

2 teaspoons grated **fresh
ginger**

1 teaspoon **sesame oil**

2 teaspoons packed **light
brown sugar**

Mix together the marinade ingredients in a small bowl
and stir until the sugar has dissolved. Pour half into a
shallow nonreactive dish, reserving the remainder in a
bowl to use as a dressing. Add the tuna to the dish and
turn to coat in the marinade, then let marinate for about
15 minutes.

Meanwhile, using a spiralizer fitted with a ⅛ inch
spaghetti blade, spiralize the cucumber and carrot.

Put the spiralized vegetables into a bowl with the lettuce
and scallions.

Heat a ridged grill pan over high heat. Remove the
tuna from the marinade, add to the pan, and cook for
2–3 minutes on each side or until the outside is cooked
but the middle is still pink, brushing with any remaining
marinade from the dish.

Pour the reserved dressing over the carrot and
cucumber salad. Toss well, then divide between 2 plates.
Top the salad with the tuna steaks, sprinkle with the
sesame seeds, and serve immediately.

For seared sesame tuna salad, rub each tuna steak
with 2 teaspoons miso paste, then pat 2 tablespoons
sesame seeds on each to coat. Heat 1 tablespoon
sunflower oil in a skillet over medium heat, then cook
as above and set aside. Put the spiralized carrot and
cucumber into a bowl with the scallions. In a small bowl,
mix together 1 tablespoon soy sauce, the finely grated
zest and juice of 1 unwaxed lime, and 2 teaspoons
ginger paste. Pour the dressing over the vegetables
and stir well to coat. Divide the salad between 2 plates.
Slice the tuna and arrange on top.

smoked salmon salad

Serves **4**

Preparation time **10 minutes, plus marinating**

1 large **fennel bulb**, ends trimmed

1 **zucchini**, ends trimmed and halved widthwise

½ **cucumber**, ends trimmed and halved widthwise

2 teaspoons finely chopped **dill**

2 tablespoons **lemon juice**

1 tablespoon **olive oil**

1 teaspoon **superfine sugar**

½ teaspoon **sea salt flakes**

8 slices **smoked salmon**

lemon wedges, to serve

Using a spiralizer fitted with a ribbon blade, spiralize the fennel, zucchini, and cucumber. Pat the cucumber dry on paper towels.

Put the spiralized vegetables into a large bowl and add the dill, lemon juice, oil, sugar, and salt. Toss well to combine and let marinate for 10 minutes.

Divide the vegetables between 4 plates, top with the salmon, and serve immediately with lemon wedges to squeeze over the salad.

For smoked salmon with pickled cucumber, using the ribbon blade, spiralize 1 cucumber. Snip any long ribbons in half with a pair of scissors. Put the spiralized cucumber into a bowl and stir in 2 tablespoons white wine vinegar, a pinch salt, and 2 tablespoons freshly chopped dill. Stir well and let marinate for 10 minutes. Halve, pit, peel, and slice 2 avocados and set aside. Divide the pickled cucumber among 4 plates and top with 7 oz smoked salmon and the sliced avocado.

mackerel & quail egg salad

Serves **4**
Preparation time **10 minutes**
Cooking time **20 minutes**

12 **quail eggs**
1½ (4 oz) packages
   watercress or **arugula**
   leaves
12 oz **smoked peppered**
   mackerel fillets, skin
   removed and broken into
   large flakes
16 **cherry tomatoes**, halved

For the crispy potato straws
2 **potatoes**, peeled and ends
   trimmed
1 tablespoon **olive oil**
salt and **black pepper**

For the dressing
2 tablespoons **olive oil**
2 teaspoons **whole-grain**
   mustard
1 tablespoon **white wine**
   vinegar
1 teaspoon **honey**
1 tablespoon chopped **chives**

First, make the crispy potato straws. Using a spiralizer fitted with a ⅛ inch spaghetti blade, spiralize the potatoes. Put the spiralized potatoes into a large bowl, add the oil, season with salt and pepper, and toss together to coat. Line a large baking sheet with parchment paper and arrange the potatoes on the baking sheet in a single layer. Bake in a preheated oven, at 350°F, for 10 minutes, then turn the potatoes, removing any potatoes that are cooked, and bake for another 10 minutes or until golden and crispy. Let cool.

Meanwhile, cook the quail eggs in a saucepan of boiling water for 3 minutes. Drain the eggs, refresh in cold water, then shell and halve them.

To make the dressing, whisk together the oil, mustard, vinegar, and honey in a small bowl. Season to taste and stir in the chives.

Toss the watercress or arugula leaves with a little of the dressing and divide among 4 plates. Top with the smoked mackerel, quail eggs, and tomatoes, drizzle with the remaining dressing, and top with the crispy potato straws. Serve immediately.

For mackerel & veg noodle salad with citrus
dressing, spiralize ½ cucumber and 2 carrots, using the spaghetti blade. Put into a large bowl with 1 sliced red bell pepper. In a small bowl, whisk together 1 tablespoon toasted sesame oil, 1½ tablespoons dark soy sauce, 1 teaspoon grated fresh ginger, 1 crushed garlic clove, and the juice of 1 tangerine. Pour the dressing over the spiralized vegetables and toss together. Divide among 4 plates and top with the flaked mackerel.

beet & smoked trout salad

Serves **2**

Preparation time **10 minutes**

2 **fresh beets**, scrubbed and
ends trimmed

2 tablespoons **reduced-fat
crème fraîche**

2 tablespoons **nonfat Greek
yogurt**

1 tablespoon **creamed
horseradish sauce**

2 teaspoons **white wine
vinegar**

1 (4 oz) package **watercress**

8 oz **hot-smoked trout fillets**,
flaked into large pieces

black pepper

Using a spiralizer fitted with a ⅛ inch spaghetti blade,
spiralize the beets.

Mix together the crème fraîche, yogurt, horseradish
sauce and vinegar in a large bowl. Add the spiralized
beets and gently stir until evenly coated.

Divide the watercress between 2 plates, top with the
beets, and arrange the trout over the top. Sprinkle with
some pepper and serve immediately.

For beet & bresaola salad, spiralize 2 beets as above.
In a large bowl, mix together 3 tablespoons reduced-
fat crème fraîche, 1 tablespoon creamed horseradish
sauce, 2 teaspoons red wine vinegar, and 2 teaspoons
olive oil. Season well. Stir in the spiralized beets and
1 (4 oz) package arugula leaves. Divide 2 oz thinly
sliced bresaola between 2 plates, then add the beets.
Serve immediately.

mains

asian steamed chicken dumplings

Serves **2**
Preparation time **15 minutes**
Cooking time **15 minutes**

2 **zucchini**, ends trimmed and halved widthwise
1 **carrot**, peeled, ends trimmed, and halved widthwise
2 tablespoons **toasted peanuts**, coarsely chopped
finely grated zest and juice of
  1 **unwaxed lime**
⅓ cup **sweet chili sauce**
½ teaspoon **Thai fish sauce**

For the dumplings
2 **scallions**, coarsely chopped
1 inch piece **fresh ginger**, peeled and chopped
1 **red chili,** seeded and chopped
1 small bunch of **fresh cilantro**
1 large boneless, skinless **chicken breast** (about 7 oz), cut into chunks
1 teaspoon **light soy sauce**

First, make the dumplings. Put the scallions, ginger, chili, and cilantro into a food processor and process until finely chopped. Add the chicken and soy sauce and pulse until combined. Transfer the mixture to a bowl and shape into 12 small balls, using wet hands.

Place the dumplings in a steamer over a saucepan of simmering water and steam for about 15 minutes or until cooked through.

Meanwhile, using a spiralizer fitted with a ⅛ inch spaghetti blade, spiralize the zucchini and carrot.

Put the spiralized vegetables into a bowl with the peanuts. Mix together the lime zest and juice, sweet chili sauce, and fish sauce in a separate small bowl, then pour over the zucchini and carrot, reserving a little. Stir well to coat the vegetables in the dressing.

Divide the vegetables between 2 plates and top with the chicken dumplings. Pour over the reserved dressing and serve immediately.

For chicken in miso vegetable noodle broth, put 2½ cups hot chicken broth into a saucepan, then stir in 2 tablespoons white miso paste and 2 teaspoons grated fresh ginger. Add 1 boneless, skinless chicken breast, bring to a boil, cover, and simmer for 10 minutes. Meanwhile, spiralize 2 carrots and 2 zucchini, using the spaghetti blade. Remove the chicken from the broth and shred into pieces, then return to the pan with the spiralized zucchini and carrots. Simmer for another 3–4 minutes, until tender. Garnish with shredded scallions.

beet, quinoa & feta burgers

Makes **4**
Preparation time **10 minutes,
plus chilling**
Cooking time **12–15 minutes**

1 **fresh beet**, scrubbed and
ends trimmed
1 **carrot**, peeled, ends
trimmed, and halved
widthwise
⅔ cup cooked **quinoa**
½ cup chopped **walnuts**
¼ cup chopped **mint**
juice of ½ **lemon**
2 teaspoons **harissa paste**
2 tablespoons **whole-wheat
flour**
¾ cup crumbled **feta cheese**
1 extra-large **egg**, beaten
salt and **black pepper**
1 tablespoon **sunflower oil**,
for brushing

To serve
Greek yogurt
1 teaspoon **harissa paste**
mixed salad greens
tomatoes

Using a spiralizer fitted with a ⅛ inch spaghetti blade,
spiralize the beet and carrot. Coarsely snip any long
spirals in half with a pair of scissors.

Put the spiralized vegetables into a bowl, add the quinoa,
walnuts, mint, lemon juice, harissa paste, flour, and feta,
and stir together. Mix in the egg and season well with
salt and pepper. Transfer the mixture to a plate, cover,
and chill in the refrigerator for 30 minutes.

Divide the mixture into 4 portions and shape into
patties, using your hands. Put them onto a nonstick
baking sheet and brush with a little oil. Cook them under
a preheated hot broiler for 6–7 minutes on each side or
until cooked through.

Top the burgers with spoonfuls of yogurt drizzled with
the harissa and serve with salad greens and tomatoes.

For hamburgers with beet, spiralize 2 beets as above,
snipping any extra long spirals in half with a pair of
scissors. Put the spiralized beets into a bowl and add
1 lb lean ground beef. Stir in 2 tablespoons creamed
horseradish, 1 tablespoon Worcestershire sauce, and
1 egg yolk. Season well, then divide into 4 portions and
shape into patties. Cook the patties as above. Serve in
burger buns with watercress.

vegetable biryani with cauli-rice

Serves **4**
Preparation time **10 minutes**
Cooking time **10 minutes**

4 cups **cauliflower florets**
1 small **onion**, ends trimmed
1 large **carrot**, peeled, ends
  trimmed, and halved widthwise
1 **zucchini**, ends trimmed and
  halved widthwise
1 tablespoon **sunflower oil**
2 teaspoons **black mustard
  seeds**
5 **cardamom pods**, crushed
2 tablespoons **medium curry
  powder**
1 **cinnamon stick**
6 **curry leaves**
1 inch piece **fresh ginger**,
  peeled and finely grated
1 **green chili,** seeded and
  finely chopped
1 **garlic clove**, crushed
⅔ cup **vegetable broth**
2 **tomatoes**, chopped
salt and **black pepper**
2 tablespoons chopped **fresh
  cilantro**
¼ cup **toasted almonds**

Put the cauliflower into a food processor and pulse until it resembles rice. Set aside.

Using a spiralizer fitted with a ⅛ inch spaghetti blade, spiralize the onion and set aside. Change to a ribbon blade and spiralize the carrot and zucchini. Coarsely snip any long ribbons in half with a pair of scissors.

Heat the oil in a large skillet or wok over medium heat. Stir in the spices and curry leaves and cook for 1 minute or until the mustard seeds start to pop. Stir in the spiralized onion, the ginger, chili, garlic, and 2 tablespoons of the broth and cook for 3–4 minutes, until the onion has softened.

Add the cauliflower rice and stir to coat in the spices, then add the spiralized carrot and zucchini and the tomatoes. Stir well, then pour in the remaining broth. Cook for 5 minutes or until the liquid has evaporated and the vegetables are tender, stirring occasionally. Season to taste with salt and pepper.

Divide the biryani among 4 bowls and sprinkle with cilantro and toasted almonds.

For turkey biriyani, prepare the cauliflower rice and spiralize 1 small onion and 1 large carrot as above. Heat the oil in a large skillet as above, add the spiralized onion, and stir in 1 lb ground turkey. Cook over medium heat for 4–5 minutes, until the onion has browned. Stir in 2 tablespoons medium curry paste, the cauliflower rice, spiralized carrot, chopped tomatoes, and ⅔ cup chicken broth, then cook as above. Serve with a handful of chopped cashews.

butternut squash & goat cheese tart

Serves **6–8**
Preparation time **10 minutes**
Cooking time **1 hour**

½ **butternut squash** (the
   nonbulbous end), peeled
   and halved widthwise
1 tablespoon **olive oil**
4 **smoked bacon slices**,
   chopped
1 **garlic clove**, crushed
8 inch **frozen pie crust** (cook
   from frozen)
5 oz **goat cheese**, coarsely
   chopped
1¼ cups **heavy cream**
3 **eggs**
8 **sage leaves**
salt and **black pepper**

Using a spiralizer fitted with a ⅛ inch spaghetti blade, spiralize the squash.

Heat the oil in a large skillet and cook the bacon over medium heat for 2–3 minutes, until browned. Add the garlic and cook for 1 minute, then add the squash and stir-fry for 2–3 minutes, until slightly softened. Arrange the squash mixture in the frozen pie crust and sprinkle with half the goat cheese.

Beat together the cream and eggs in a bowl, then season with salt and pepper. Pour the egg mixture over the butternut squash. Sprinkle with the remaining goat cheese and the sage leaves.

Bake in a preheated oven, at 375°F, for 40 minutes, until the top is golden and the filling set. Let cool for 5 minutes, then cut the tart into slices and serve.

For butternut squash & feta tart, prepare and bake the tart as above, replacing the goat cheese with 1 cup crumbled feta cheese. Serve the tart topped with a large handful of arugula leaves.

zoodles with crab, chili & lemon

Serves **2**
Preparation time **5 minutes**
Cooking time **5 minutes**

2 large **zucchini**, ends trimmed
    and halved widthwise
1 tablespoon **olive oil**
1 **garlic clove,** crushed
1 small **red chili,** seeded and
    finely chopped
3½ oz **white crabmeat**
finely grated zest and juice of
    ½ **unwaxed lemon**
1 tablespoon chopped **mint**
black pepper

Using a spiralizer fitted with a ⅛ inch spaghetti blade,
spiralize the zucchini.

Heat the oil in a wok or large skillet, add the garlic and
chili, and cook gently over medium heat for 2 minutes.
Stir in the spiralized zucchini and cook for 2–3 minutes,
until just tender. Stir in the crab, lemon zest and juice,
and mint, gently toss together, and season with pepper.
Serve immediately.

For zoodles with garlic clams, prepare the spiralized
zucchini as above. Heat 1 tablespoon olive oil in a wok or
large skillet and add 2 finely chopped garlic cloves and a
pinch of dried chili flakes. Add 1 lb small cleaned clams
and pour in ½ cup dry white wine. Cover with a lid and
cook for 2–3 minutes, until the clams open (discarding
any that do not open). Stir in the spiralized zucchini and
2 tablespoons chopped parsley. Cook for 2 minutes, then
divide between 2 bowls. Serve with lemon wedges to
squeeze over the top.

baked chicken & sweet potatoes

Serves **4**
Preparation time **10 minutes**
Cooking time **30–35 minutes**

finely grated zest and juice
    of 2 **unwaxed lemons**,
    reserving the squeezed
    lemon halves
1 tablespoon **dried oregano**
2 teaspoons **dried thyme**
2 teaspoons **smoked paprika**
scant ½ cup **white wine** or
    chicken broth
2 tablespoons **olive oil**
2 **sweet potatoes** (about
    13 oz) peeled and ends
    trimmed
4 **chicken thighs**
4 **chicken drumsticks**
6 **garlic cloves**, unpeeled
14 **pitted green olives**
salt and **black pepper**
steamed green beans or
    broccoli, to serve

Mix together the lemon zest and juice, dried herbs, paprika, white wine or broth, and olive oil in a small bowl and season well with salt and pepper.

Using a spiralizer fitted with a ⅛ inch spaghetti blade, spiralize the sweet potatoes.

Put the chicken, spiralized sweet potatoes, and garlic cloves into a large roasting pan. Pour the lemony mixture over the chicken and potatoes and mix everything together until well coated. Arrange the chicken pieces, skin side up, on the top of the sweet potatoes and tuck in the reserved squeezed lemon halves.

Bake in a preheated oven, at 375°F, for 20 minutes. Baste the chicken and sweet potatoes with the lemony sauce and add the olives. Return to the oven and cook for another 10–15 minutes, until the chicken is golden brown and the sweet potatoes are tender. Serve with some steamed green beans or broccoli.

For baked Moroccan chicken & sweet potatoes,
make the baked chicken and sweet potatoes as above, replacing the herbs and paprika with 2 teaspoons harissa paste and using scant ½ cup chicken broth. Remove from the oven and sprinkle with ½ cup pomegranate seeds and 2 tablespoons chopped mint.

shrimp pad thai

Serves **2**
Preparation time **15 minutes**
Cooking time **10 minutes**

- 1 **daikon** (about 12 oz), peeled, ends trimmed, and halved widthwise
- 1 **carrot**, ends trimmed and halved widthwise
- 2 tablespoons **peanut oil**
- 1 **garlic clove**, chopped
- 1 **red chili,** seeded and finely chopped
- 1 bunch of **scallions**, sliced
- 4 oz **raw, shelled shrimp**
- 2 **eggs**, beaten
- 2 cups **bean sprouts**
- 2 tablespoons **blanched peanuts**, toasted and coarsely chopped
- ¼ cup chopped **fresh cilantro**
- 4 **lime wedges**, to serve

For the sauce
- 2 tablespoons **tamarind paste**
- 2 tablespoons **Thai fish sauce**
- 2 tablespoons packed **light brown sugar**
- juice of 1 **lime**

First, make the sauce. In a small bowl, whisk together the tamarind paste, fish sauce, sugar, and lime juice.

Using a spiralizer fitted with a ¼ inch flat noodle blade, spiralize the daikon. Change to a ⅛ inch spaghetti blade and spiralize the carrot, keeping the daikon and carrot separate.

Heat a wok over high heat, then add 1 tablespoon of the oil and swirl around. Add the garlic, chili, and scallions and stir-fry for 1 minute, stirring continuously. Add the spiralized daikon and stir-fry for 2 minutes, then add the spiralized carrots and shrimp and stir-f ry for 1–2 minutes or until the shrimp have turned pink.

Push the stir-fried ingredients to the side of the wok and add the remaining oil. Pour in the eggs and cook, stirring continuously, until they begin to set.

Add the bean sprouts and pour over the sauce, toss everything together, and heat through, stirring, for 2 minutes. Stir in half the peanuts and cilantro, then spoon into bowls and sprinkle with the remainder. Serve immediately with lime wedges to squeeze over.

For shrimp & daikon noodle salad, spiralize 1 daikon and 1 carrot, using the spaghetti blade. Put into a large bowl and add 1¼ cups bean sprouts, 5 oz cooked, shelled shrimp, and 2 tablespoons each chopped mint and fresh cilantro. In a small bowl, whisk together the grated zest and juice of 1 unwaxed lime, 1 teaspoon packed brown sugar, 2 teaspoons Thai fish sauce, ½ small red chili, seeded and finely chopped, and 2 teaspoons grated fresh ginger. Pour the dressing over the vegetables and toss together.

zoodles with avocado sauce

Serves **2**
Preparation time **10 minutes**
Cooking time **5 minutes**

2 **zucchini**, ends trimmed and
   halved widthwise
1 ripe **avocado**
1 **garlic clove**
juice of ½ **lemon**
¼ cup coarsely chopped **flat
   leaf parsley**
⅔ cup **basil leaves**
2 tablespoons **olive** or
   avocado oil
cooking spray oil, for frying
3 tablespoons **pine nuts**,
   toasted
salt and **black pepper**

Using a spiralizer fitted with a ⅛ inch spaghetti blade,
spiralize the zucchini.

Halve, pit, and peel the avocado, then put into a food
processor with the garlic, lemon juice, herbs, and olive
or avocado oil and process until smooth. Season to taste
with salt and pepper.

Spray the bottom of a nonstick skillet or wok with
spray oil and heat over medium heat. Add the spiralized
zucchini and stir-fry for 3–4 minutes, until just tender.
Remove from the heat and stir in the sauce to coat.

Divide the zoodles between 2 bowls, sprinkle with the
pine nuts and extra pepper, and serve immediately.

For an avocado and cashew nut sauce, halve, pit,
and peel 1 avocado, then put it into a food processor
with 1 garlic clove, 2 tablespoons olive oil, the juice
of ½ lemon, ½ cup cashew nuts, and ⅔ cup basil
leaves. Process until smooth and season with salt
and black pepper.

spanish chorizo tortilla

Serves **6**
Preparation time **10 minutes**
Cooking time **20–25 minutes**

1 large **onion**, ends trimmed
4 **russet potatoes**, peeled
  and ends trimmed
2 tablespoons **olive oil**
6 oz **chorizo**, diced
5 **eggs**
2 tablespoons **flat leaf**
  parsley
salt and **black pepper**
1 teaspoon **smoked paprika**,
  for sprinkling

Using a spiralizer fitted with a ⅛ inch spaghetti blade, spiralize the onion and potatoes, keeping them separate.

Heat 1 tablespoon of the olive oil in an 8 inch nonstick skillet with a lid. Gently cook the chorizo and spiralized onion over medium heat for 2–3 minutes, until the onion has softened and the paprika oil has been released from the chorizo. Add the spiralized potatoes and stir to coat in the paprika and onion mixture. Cover and cook for 5 minutes, turning the potatoes once and shaking the pan from time to time, until the potatoes are just tender.

Beat together the eggs and parsley in a large bowl and season with salt and pepper. Add the potato mixture and stir to combine. Heat the remaining oil in the skillet and pour in the egg and potato mixture. Cook over low heat for 8–10 minutes, without stirring, until set.

Place the skillet under a preheated hot broiler and cook for 2–3 minutes, until the top of the tortilla is golden brown. Transfer the tortilla to a board. Sprinkle the tortilla with the smoked paprika, cut into wedges, and serve.

For butternut squash & spinach tortilla, spiralize ½ butternut squash, peeled, using the spaghetti blade. Heat 2 tablespoons olive oil in an 8 inch nonstick skillet, stir in the spiralized squash, and cook over medium heat for 2–3 minutes, then cover and cook for 5 minutes. Add 5 cups spinach and stir until wilted. Beat together 5 eggs in a large bowl, season with salt and pepper, and stir in the squash mixture. Cook the tortilla as above.

sesame & ginger salmon

Serves **2**
Preparation time **10 minutes**
Cooking time **12–15 minutes**

1 inch piece **fresh ginger**, peeled and cut into thin matchsticks

2 tablespoons **light soy sauce**

2 tablespoons **Chinese rice wine vinegar**

1 teaspoon **toasted sesame oil**

1 **carrot**, peeled, ends trimmed, and halved widthwise

1 **zucchini**, ends trimmed and halved widthwise

4 **scallions**, thinly sliced

2 **skinless salmon fillets** (about 7 oz each)

2 teaspoons **sesame seeds**, toasted

steamed rice, to serve

Mix together the ginger, soy sauce, rice wine vinegar, and sesame oil in a small bowl to make a sauce.

Using a spiralizer fitted with a ⅛ inch spaghetti blade, spiralize the carrot and zucchini.

Put two 9 inch squares of parchment paper onto a large baking sheet. Divide the spiralized vegetables and the scallions between the 2 sheets of parchment paper and then put a salmon fillet on top of each pile of vegetables. Spoon over the sauce and sprinkle withthe sesame seeds. Fold over the paper to seal the packages.

Put the packages onto a baking sheet and bake in a preheated oven, at 400°F, for 12–15 minutes, until the salmon is opaque and the fish flakes easily. Transfer the packages to plates, carefully open up the packages, and serve with steamed rice.

For creamy salmon with asparagus & zoodles, spiralize 2 zucchini using the spaghetti blade. Cut 2 boneless, skinless salmon fillets into bite-size pieces. Cut 1½ inches off the ends of 7 oz asparagus stems, set the tips to one side, and finely chop the stems. Heat 2 teaspoons olive oil in a large skillet or wok and gently cook the salmon and chopped asparagus stems for 3–4 minutes, until the salmon is cooked and starts to flake. Meanwhile, bring a saucepan of lightly salted water to a boil, add the asparagus tips, and cook for 3 minutes, until tender, then drain. Add the spiralized zucchini to the salmon mixture and stir-fry for 2–3 minutes, until tender, then add the asparagus tips. Add ½ cup garlic and herb cream cheese and stir until the salmon and vegetables are well coated. Serve immediately.

butternut squash with ricotta

Serves **2**
Preparation time **5 minutes**
Cooking time **10 minutes**

½ **butternut squash** (the
   nonbulbous end), peeled
   and halved widthwise
½ cup **ricotta cheese**
2 tablespoons chopped **fresh
   herbs**, such as parsley,
   chives, and basil
finely grated zest and juice of
   1 small **unwaxed lemon**
1 tablespoon **sunflower oil**
1 **garlic clove**, crushed
3½ cups **baby spinach**
⅔ cup **frozen peas**
salt and **black pepper**
freshly grated **Parmesan
   cheese**, to serve

Using a spiralizer fitted with a ⅛ inch spaghetti blade,
spiralize the squash.

Mix together the ricotta, herbs, and lemon zest and juice
in a small bowl to make a sauce.

Heat the oil in a large wok or skillet over medium heat.
Add the garlic and cook for 1 minute, then stir in the
spiralized squash and stir-fry for about 5 minutes or
until the squash starts to soften but is not breaking up.
Stir in the spinach and peas and cook for 2 minutes, or
until the spinach has wilted.

Add the ricotta and herb sauce and ¼ cup boiling water,
stir, and cook for another 1−2 minutes, until the sauce
has coated the squash. Season to taste with salt and
pepper, sprinkle some Parmesan over the top, and serve
immediately.

For spicy sausage & butternut squash spaghetti,
prepare ½ butternut squash as above. Heat 1 tablespoon
olive oil in a skillet with a lid over high heat. Squeeze the
meat out of 4 Italian style link sausage skins and add to
the pan, breaking it up with the back of a wooden spoon.
Fry for a few minutes or until the meat starts to brown
and resembles coarse ground meat. Add a pinch of dried
chili flakes and 1 teaspoon fennel seeds and cook over
medium heat for about 10 minutes, or until the meat
becomes crisp, golden brown, and slightly caramelized.
Stir in ¾ cup canned, diced tomatoes and season to
taste. Stir in the spiralized squash, cover, and simmer for
4−5 minutes, until the squash is tender.

chicken chow mein

Serves **4**

Preparation time **10 minutes,
plus marinating**

Cooking time **10–15 minutes**

2 tablespoons **light soy sauce**

2 tablespoons **dry sherry**
or **Chinese cooking wine
(Shaoxing)**

3 tablespoons **oyster sauce**

½ teaspoon **toasted sesame
oil**

2 teaspoons **cornstarch**

3 boneless, skinless **chicken
breasts**, cut into thin strips

1 large **carrot**, peeled,
ends trimmed, and halved
widthwise

1 **daikon** (about 1 lb), peeled,
ends trimmed, and halved
widthwise

1 tablespoon **sunflower oil**

1 **garlic clove**, crushed

2 teaspoons grated **fresh
ginger**

1 bunch of **scallions**, sliced

2 cups **snow peas**

1¼ cups **bean sprouts**

Mix together 1 tablespoon each of the soy sauce, sherry or Chinese cooking wine, and oyster sauce, the sesame oil, and 1 teaspoon of the cornstarch in a large bowl. Add the chicken, stir to coat in the marinade, then cover and let marinate in the refrigerator for 20 minutes.

Mix together the remaining soy sauce, sherry or Chinese cooking wine, oyster sauce, and cornstarch in a small bowl and set aside.

Using a spiralizer fitted with a ¼ inch flat noodle blade, spiralize the carrot, keeping it separate. Change to a ⅛ inch spaghetti blade and spiralize the daikon.

Heat the sunflower oil in a wok or large skillet over high heat until hot. Add the marinated chicken and stir-fry for 3–4 minutes, until lightly browned. Add the garlic, ginger, and scallions and stir-fry for 2–3 minutes. Add the spiralized vegetables and the snow peas and stir-fry for another 3–4 minutes, until the vegetables are just tender and the chicken is cooked through. Add the bean sprouts and reserved sauce and stir until the sauce has thickened and coated all the ingredients. Serve immediately.

For speedy beef chow mein, prepare the spiralized vegetables as above but not the sauce. Make the chow mein as above, replacing the chicken with 1 lb sirloin steak, cut into thin strips, and replacing the sauce with 1¾ cups store-bought stir-fry sauce. After stirring in the sauce, cook for another 2–3 minutes, until the sauce has heated through and coated all the ingredients.

turkey bolognese with zoodles

Serves **4**
Preparation time **10 minutes**
Cooking time **25–35 minutes**

3 **zucchini** (ideally yellow
zucchini), ends trimmed and
halved widthwise
1 large **onion**, ends trimmed
1 large **carrot**, peeled,
ends trimmed, and halved
widthwise
14½ oz **lean ground turkey**
1 **garlic clove**, crushed
8 oz **closed cup** or **cremini
mushrooms**, sliced
1 teaspoon **paprika**
⅔ cup **red wine** or **beef broth**
1 (14½ oz) can **diced
tomatoes**
1 tablespoon **tomato paste**
2 teaspoons **dried mixed
herbs**
salt and **black pepper**
freshly grated **Parmesan
cheese**, to serve

Using a spiralizer fitted with a ⅛ inch spaghetti blade,
spiralize the zucchini and onion, keeping them separate.
Change to a ribbon blade and spiralize the carrot. Snip
any really long ribbons in half with a pair of scissors.

Put the turkey, spiralized onion, and garlic into a
large, nonstick saucepan and dry-fry over high heat
for 3–4 minutes, until lightly browned. Stir in the
spiralized carrot, mushrooms, and paprika and cook
for 2–3 minutes. Stir in the red wine or broth and cook
for 2–3 minutes, until the liquid has reduced, then stir in
the tomatoes, tomato paste, and mixed herbs. Reduce
the heat, cover, and simmer for 15–20 minutes, stirring
occasionally, until the sauce has reduced and thickened.

Season to taste with salt and pepper, then stir in the
spiralized zucchini and cook, uncovered, for 2–3 minutes
or until the zucchini is al dente. Serve sprinkled with a
little Parmesan.

For mushroom bolognese with zoodles, spiralize
3 zucchini, 1 onion, and 1 carrot as above. Heat
2 tablespoons olive oil in a large saucepan, add the
spiralized onion, carrot, and 2 crushed garlic cloves.
Cook over low heat for 8 minutes, until the vegetables
have softened. Increase the heat and add 1 lb mixed
mushrooms, chopped. Cook for 3–4 minutes, then stir
in the red wine, diced tomatoes, tomatoe paste, and
herbs, as above. Stir in 1 teaspoon balsamic vinegar,
bring to a boil, cover, and simmer for 30 minutes, stirring
occasionally, until the mushrooms are tender and the
sauce has thickened. Season to taste, then stir in the
spiralized zucchini and cook as above. Serve sprinkled
with a little grated Parmesan.

miso-baked cod & daikon noodles

Serves **2**

Preparation time **15 minutes, plus marinating**

Cooking time **14–17 minutes**

2 chunky **cod loins** (about 7 oz each)

sunflower oil, for oiling

¾ **daikon** (about 8 oz), peeled, ends trimmed, and halved widthwise

3 tablespoons **black sesame seeds**

½ teaspoon **superfine sugar**

1 tablespoon **seasoned soy sauce**

1 tablespoon **liquid dashi**

1 teaspoon **yuzu juice**

10 oz **choy sum** and **bok choy**, stems trimmed and leaves cut into chunks

For the marinade

2 tablespoons **white miso paste**

3 tablespoons **sake**

1 **garlic clove**, crushed

1 inch piece **fresh ginger**, peeled and finely grated

1 tablespoon **superfine sugar**

2 teaspoons **mirin**

Mix together the marinade ingredients in a shallow dish, add the cod, and coat in the marinade. Cover and let marinate in the refrigerator for 2–3 hours or overnight.

Lightly oil a baking sheet. Using a spiralizer fitted with a ¼ inch flat noodle blade, spiralize the daikon.

Put the fish onto the prepared baking sheet and spoon over 1 tablespoon of the marinade. Bake in a preheated oven, at 350°F, for 10–12 minutes.

Preheat the broiler to high. Remove the fish from the oven, spoon the remaining marinade over the fish, and broil for 4–5 minutes, until golden brown and cooked through.

Meanwhile, toast the sesame seeds in a dry skillet for 2–3 minutes. Transfer to a mortar and pestle and grind to nearly a paste but still retaining some texture. Add the sugar, soy sauce, dashi, and yuzu juice and grind to incorporate all the flavors.

Put the spiralized daikon and the choy sum and bok choy into a steamer over a saucepan of boiling water. Steam for 3–4 minutes, until tender.

Divide the daikon noodles and greens between 2 plates and drizzle with the sesame seed dressing. Top with the cod and serve immediately.

For daikon rice with scallions, using a ⅛ inch spaghetti blade, spiralize ¾ daikon. Put the spiralized daikon into a food processor and pulse until it resembles rice. Heat 1 tablespoon coconut oil in a skillet, add 4 finely chopped scallions, and cook for 2 minutes, then stir in the rice. Stir-fry for 2–3 minutes, until just tender.

plantain, chicken & coconut curry

Serves **4**
Preparation time **10 minutes**
Cooking time **30 minutes**

2 **green plantains** (the straightest ones you can find)
1 **onion**, ends trimmed
2 tablespoons **peanut oil**
1 **garlic clove**, crushed
1 inch piece **fresh ginger**, grated
1 tablespoon **medium curry powder**
3 boneless, skinless **chicken breasts**, cut into chunks
1⅔ cups **coconut milk**
1¼ cups **chicken broth**
finely grated zest and juice of **2 unwaxed limes**
1 (7 oz) package **baby spinach**
salt and **black pepper**

To serve
naan or **other flatbread**
2 **limes**, halved

Cut the plantains in half widthwise. Score the outside of the skins and peel off, then trim the ends. Using a spiralizer fitted with a ⅛ inch spaghetti blade, spiralize the plantains and onion, keeping them separate.

Heat 1 tablespoon of the oil in a large saucepan, add the spiralized onion, garlic, and ginger, and cook gently over medium heat for 3–4 minutes, until softened. Add the curry powder and cook for 1 minute, then stir in the chicken and cook for 3–4 minutes, until lightly browned. Stir in the coconut milk and broth, bring to a boil, then cover and simmer for 15 minutes. Season to taste with salt and pepper. Stir in most of the spiralized plantain, reserving a handful to fry later. Cover the pan and simmer for 5–6 minutes, until just tender. Remove the saucepan from the heat. Stir in the lime zest and juice and spinach, cover, and let stand for 2–3 minutes, until the spinach is wilted.

Meanwhile, heat the remaining oil in a small skillet and cook the reserved spiralized plantain over medium heat for 2–3 minutes, until crisp.

Spoon the curry into bowls and sprinkle with the crispy plantain. Serve immediately with naan or other flatbread and lime halves to squeeze over the top.

For Thai red chicken & plantain curry, prepare and cook the curry as above, replacing the curry powder with 2 tablespoons Thai red curry paste, 1 trimmed and chopped lemon grass stalk, and 2 torn kaffir lime leaves. Stir in 1 teaspoon Thai fish sauce at the end of the cooking time. Serve with steamed rice.

chicken & chorizo jambalaya

Serves **4**

Preparation time **10 minutes**

Cooking time **15–18 minutes**

2 large **carrots**, peeled, ends trimmed, and halved widthwise

1 **onion**, ends trimmed

1 teaspoon **sunflower oil**

3½ oz **chorizo**, chopped

3 boneless, skinless **chicken breasts**, cut into small cubes

1 tablespoon **Cajun seasoning**

1 **red bell pepper**, cored, seeded, and diced

1 **green bell pepper**, cored, seeded, and diced

1 (14½ oz) can **diced tomatoes**

⅓ cup **frozen peas**

6 **scallions**, chopped

3½ oz **cooked, shelled shrimp**

Using a spiralizer fitted with a ⅛ inch spaghetti blade, spiralize the carrots and onion, keeping them separate. Put the spiralized carrots into a food processor and pulse until the mixture resembles rice.

Heat the oil in a large skillet, add the chorizo and spiralized onion, and cook over medium heat for 3–4 minutes, until the onion has softened and the paprika oil has been released from the chorizo. Add the chicken and Cajun spice and cook for 3–4 minutes, until the chicken is lightly browned. Stir in the bell peppers and cook for 2 minutes, then add the carrot rice, tomatoes, peas, and scallions, reserving a few scallions for garnish. Stir to combine.

Simmer for 5 minutes, stirring occasionally. Stir in the shrimp and cook for 2 minutes, or until the vegetables are tender and the chicken is cooked through. Serve sprinkled with the reserved scallions.

For seafood paella, prepare the spiralized carrot and onion as above. Heat 1 tablespoon olive oil in a large skillet, add the onion and 1 crushed garlic clove, then stir in 1 teaspoon smoked paprika and ½ teaspoon ground turmeric. Add the carrot rice, 1 (14½ oz) can diced tomatoes, ⅓ cup frozen peas, and 2 tablespoons lemon juice. Stir to combine. Simmer for 5 minutes, then stir in 13 oz defrosted, frozen cooked mixed seafood. Simmer for 2–3 minutes, until heated through, then stir in 2 tablespoons chopped parsley.

butternut squash spaghetti

Serves **4**
Preparation time **10 minutes**
Cooking time **10 minutes**

½ large **butternut squash** (the
   nonbulbous end), peeled and
   cut in half widthwise
2 teaspoons **olive oil**
black pepper

**For the arugula & walnut
   pesto**
3¾ cups **arugula leaves**, plus
   extra to garnish
1 **garlic clove**
½ cup **walnut halves**
¼ cup **grated Parmesan
   cheese**
juice of ½ **lemon**
¼ cup **extra virgin olive oil**

First, make the pesto. Put the arugula, garlic, walnuts, Parmesan, and lemon juice into a food processor and process until finely chopped—you may need to scrape the mixture down the sides of the food processor with a rubber spatula from time to time. With the motor still running, gradually add the extra virgin olive oil through the funnel until combined.

Using a spiralizer fitted with a ⅛ inch spaghetti blade, spiralize the squash.

Heat the olive oil in a large wok or skillet, add the spiralized squash, and stir-fry for 5–7 minutes, until softened but not broken up. Stir in the pesto until the squash spaghetti is well coated. Season with pepper, garnish with a few arugula leaves, and serve immediately.

For butternut squash spaghetti with spinach and pistachio pesto, prepare and cook the butternut squash spaghetti as above, omitting the arugula and walnut pesto. Meanwhile, put 3 cups spinach leaves into a food processor with 1 garlic clove, ⅓ cup pistachios, ¼ cup grated Parmesan cheese, and the juice of ½ lemon in a food processor and process until finely chopped, then, with the motor still running, gradually add ¼ cup extra virgin olive oil through the funnel until combined. When the squash spaghetti is cooked, stir in the pesto until the squash is well coated. Serve immediately.

moroccan turkey burgers

Serves **6**
Preparation time **10 minutes,
  plus chilling**
Cooking time **15 minutes**

For the burgers
1 large **zucchini**, ends trimmed
  and halved widthwise
1lb **lean ground turkey** or
  chicken breast
4 **scallions**, chopped
1 **garlic clove**, crushed
2 tablespoons chopped **mint**
2 tablespoons chopped **fresh
  cilantro**
1 tablespoon **harissa paste**
2 teaspoons **ground cumin**
1 **egg**, beaten
1 teaspoon **salt**
black pepper
1 tablespoon **sunflower oil**,
  for brushing

For the sumac yogurt dip
¾ cup **nonfat Greek yogurt**
1 **garlic clove**, crushed
grated zest and juice of
  ½ **unwaxed lemon**
1 tablespoon **sumac**

Using a spiralizer fitted with a ⅛ inch spaghetti blade, spiralize the zucchini.

Put all the burger ingredients into a large bowl and use your hands to mix the ingredients together. Divide the mixture into 6 portions and shape into large patties. Transfer the patties to a plate and chill in the refrigerator for 15 minutes.

Put the patties onto a nonstick baking sheet and brush them with a little oil. Cook under a preheated hot broiler for 6–7 minutes on each side, until cooked through.

While the burgers are cooking, make the dip. Put all the ingredients into a small bowl, mix together, and season to taste.

Serve the burgers hot with the sumac yogurt dip.

For herbed lamb burgers, spiralize 1 zucchini as above. Put 1 lb lean ground lamb into a large bowl with ¼ cup chopped mint, 4 chopped scallions, 1 garlic clove, grated zest 1 unwaxed lemon, 1 beaten egg, and the spiralized zucchini. Season well with salt and pepper and mix. Shape into patties and cook as above. Serve in lightly toasted pita pockets with lettuce and chopped tomatoes.

beef, zoodles & cheese lasagne

Serves **4**

Preparation time **15 minutes**

Cooking time **50–55 minutes**

4 large **zucchini**, ends trimmed and halved widthwise

1 tablespoon **olive oil**

1 **onion**, ends trimmed

1 **carrot**, peeled, ends trimmed, and halved widthwise

1 lb **lean ground beef**

1 **garlic clove**, crushed

scant ½ cup **red wine**

1 (14½ oz) can **diced tomatoes**

2 tablespoons **tomato paste**

2 teaspoons **dried mixed herbs**

1½ cups **ricotta cheese**

1 cup grated **Parmesan cheese**

8 oz **mozzarella cheese**, sliced

salt and **black pepper**

Line 2 large baking sheets with parchment paper.

Using a spiralizer fitted with a ribbon blade, spiralize the zucchini. Put the spiralized zucchini into a large bowl, add the oil and a little salt, and toss to coat in the oil and seasoning.

Spread out the zucchini in a single layer on the baking sheets and bake in a preheated oven, at 350°F, for 20 minutes, turning the zucchini and swapping over the baking sheets in the oven halfway through the cooking time. Remove from the oven and pat dry with paper towels. Set aside.

Meanwhile, using the ⅛ inch spaghetti blade, spiralize the onion and carrot, keeping them separate.

Put the beef, onion, and garlic into a large saucepan and dry-fry over medium heat for 3–4 minutes, until the meat is browned. Add the spiralized carrot and pour over the wine. Simmer for 2 minutes, then add the tomatoes, tomato paste, and herbs and season with salt and pepper. Bring to a boil, then reduce the heat, cover, and simmer for 15 minutes or until the sauce has reduced and is thick.

Beat together the ricotta with ¾ cup of the Parmesan in a small bowl.

Spread half the meat sauce over the bottom of a 1¼ quart ovenproof dish, add half the zucchini, cover with the mozzarella, and top with the remaining meat and zucchini. Spread the ricotta mixture over the top, then sprinkle with the remaining Parmesan.

Bake in the oven for 30–35 minutes, until golden and bubbling. Let stand for 5 minutes before serving.

thai green chicken curry

Serves **4**

Preparation time **5 minutes**

Cooking time **18–20 minutes**

½ **butternut squash** (the nonbulbous end), peeled and halved widthwise

1 **zucchini**, ends trimmed and halved widthwise

2 teaspoons **peanut** or **vegetable oil**

2 tablespoons **Thai green curry paste**

3 boneless, skinless **chicken breasts**, cut into thin strips

1⅔ cups **coconut milk**

1 **lemon grass stalk**, tough outer layers removed and coarsely chopped

2 **kaffir lime leaves**, thinly sliced

2 teaspoons **Thai fish sauce**

handful of **Thai basil** or **cilantro leaves**

Using a spiralizer fitted with a ¼ inch flat noodle blade, spiralize the butternut squash and zucchini, keeping them separate.

Heat the oil in a saucepan, add the Thai green curry paste, and cook for 1–2 minutes, stirring constantly. Stir in the chicken and cook for 2–3 minutes, until lightly browned. Add the coconut milk, lemon grass, lime leaves, and fish sauce. Bring to a boil, then reduce the heat and simmer for about 8 minutes, until the sauce has reduced slightly.

Stir in the spiralized squash, cover, and simmer for about 3 minutes, then stir in the spiralized zucchini. Cover and simmer for another 2–3 minutes, until the vegetables are just tender and the chicken is cooked through. Stir in the basil or cilantro and serve immediately.

For homemade Thai green curry paste, put 15 small green chilies, 4 coarsely chopped garlic cloves, 2 finely chopped lemon grass stalks, 2 torn kaffir lime leaves, 2 chopped shallots, 1 inch piece fresh ginger or galangal, 2 teaspoons black peppercorns, ½ teaspoon salt, and 1 tablespoon peanut oil into a food processor or blender and process to a thick paste. Transfer to a screw-top jar. Makes about ⅔ cup of paste, which can be stored in the refrigerator for up to 3 weeks.

mexican spicy bean burgers

Serves **4**

Preparation time **15 minutes, plus chilling**

Cooking time **15–20 minutes**

1 **onion**, ends trimmed

1 large **sweet potato,** peeled, ends trimmed, and halved widthwise

1 tablespoon **sunflower oil**

1 **green chili,** seeded and finely chopped

2 teaspoons **Mexican** or **fajita spice mix**

1 (15 oz) can **red kidney beans**, drained and rinsed

¼ cup chopped **fresh cilantro**

1 **egg**

2 teaspoons **chipotle paste**

salt and **black pepper**

To serve

4 **flour tortillas**

crisp green lettuce

fresh tomato salsa

guacamole

4 **lime wedges**

Using a spiralizer fitted with a ⅛ inch spaghetti blade, spiralize the onion and sweet potato, keeping them separate.

Heat the oil in a skillet and cook the spiralized onion and chili over medium heat for 2–3 minutes, until softened. Stir in the spice mix and cook for 1 minute. Add the spiralized sweet potato and stir-fry for 4–5 minutes, until softened. Let cool slightly.

Mash the kidney beans in a large bowl with a potato masher or fork, then add the cilantro and season well with salt and pepper. Stir in the sweet potato mixture.

Beat together the egg with the chipotle paste in a small bowl. Pour over the sweet potato and bean mixture and mix well with a fork. Divide the mixture into 4 portions and shape into patties, using your hands. Transfer the patties to a plate and chill in the refrigerator for 15 minutes.

Place the patties on a nonstick baking sheet and cook under a preheated medium-hot broiler for 4–5 minutes on each side, until golden and cooked through.

Warm the tortillas. Top each tortilla with some lettuce, a spoonful of salsa, and a burger and finish with a spoonful of guacamole. Serve with lime wedges to squeeze over.

For homemade guacamole, put 1 halved, pitted, peeled, and diced avocado into a food processor or mortar and pestle with 1 garlic clove, 1 seeded and chopped red chili, the juice of 1 unwaxed lime, 1 tablespoon chopped fresh cilantro, and salt and black pepper. Process or pound until fairly smooth and transfer to a bowl. Stir in 1 seeded and chopped tomato.

salmon teriyaki & zoodles

Serves **2**

Preparation time **10 minutes, plus marinating**

Cooking time **10–12 minutes**

2 boneless, skinless **salmon fillets** (about 5 oz each)

2 **zucchini**, ends trimmed, and halved widthwise

2 teaspoons **sesame oil**

1 cup **frozen edamame (soybeans)**

2 teaspoons **sesame seeds**

For the marinade

2 tablespoons **dark soy sauce**

1 tablespoon **mirin** or **rice wine vinegar**

1 tablespoon **honey**

1 **garlic clove**, crushed

2 teaspoons finely grated **fresh ginger**

Mix together all the marinade ingredients in a shallow, nonreactive dish, then add the salmon fillets, turn to coat, and let marinate for 15 minutes.

Meanwhile, line a baking sheet with nonstick parchment paper. Using a spiralizer fitted with a ¼ inch flat noodle blade, spiralize the zucchini. Set aside.

Put the salmon onto the prepared baking sheet and spoon over some of the marinade. Bake in a preheated oven, at 400°F, for 5 minutes. Spoon over the remaining marinade, return to the oven, and cook for another 5–7 minutes, until the salmon is opaque and the fish flakes easily.

Toward the end of the cooking time, heat the sesame oil in a wok or large skillet, add the spiralized zucchini, edamame, and sesame seeds, and stir-fry for 3–4 minutes, until the zucchini is just tender.

Divide the zucchini and edamame between 2 plates, place a salmon fillet on top of each, and spoon over any remaining sauce from the baking sheet. Serve immediately.

For chicken teriyaki, prepare and cook the dish as above, replacing the salmon with 2 boneless, skinless chicken breasts, and increasing the cooking time to 15 minutes or until the chicken is cooked through, spooning over the remaining marinade half way through the cooking time. Slice the chicken and serve it on top of the noodles.

beef & broccoli stir-fry

Serves **4**
Preparation time **10 minutes,
  plus marinating**
Cooking time **10 minutes**

1 inch piece **fresh ginger**,
  peeled and cut into thin
  strips
1 **garlic clove**, crushed
1 teaspoon **cornstarch**
2 tablespoons **dark soy sauce**
2 tablespoons **sherry** or
  **Chinese cooking wine
  (Shaoxing)**
1 lb **sirloin steak**, trimmed of
  fat and cut into thin strips
2 **carrots**, peeled, ends
  trimmed, and halved
  widthwise
1 small head of **broccoli**
1 tablespoon **sunflower oil**
½ cup **cashew nuts**, toasted
2 cups cooked **egg noodles**
2 tablespoons **oyster sauce**
scant ½ cup **beef broth** or
  water

Mix together the ginger, garlic, cornstarch, and
1 tablespoon each of soy sauce and sherry or Chinese
cooking wine in a large bowl. Stir in the beef and let
marinate for 15 minutes.

Using a spiralizer fitted with a ⅛ inch spaghetti blade,
spiralize the carrots. Change to a ¼ inch flat noodle
blade, cut the broccoli stem away from the florets, and
spiralize the stem. Break the rest of the broccoli into
small florets.

Bring a large saucepan of water to a boil and cook the
broccoli florets for 2 minutes. Drain and plunge into cold
water to stop the cooking process. Drain again and pat
dry with paper towels.

Heat 2 teaspoons of the oil in a wok over high heat until
really hot. Add the beef strips and marinade and stir-fry
for 2–3 minutes, until the beef has browned. Remove
the beef from the pan with a slotted spoon, transfer to
a plate, and set aside.

Add the remaining oil to the wok. When the oil is hot,
add the spiralized carrots and broccoli stem, the broccoli
florets, and cashew nuts, and cook for 2–3 minutes, until
the vegetables are just tender.

Return the beef and any meat juices to the wok. Add the
noodles and stir in the remaining soy sauce and sherry
or Chinese cooking wine, the oyster sauce, and broth
or water. Cook, stirring constantly, until the sauce has
coated all the ingredients. Serve immediately.

cod fish cakes

Serves **4**
Preparation time **20 minutes**
Cooking time **30–35 minutes**

8 oz skinless and boneless
cod fillets
2 large **Yukon Gold potatoes**,
peeled and ends trimmed
2 tablespoons chopped
parsley
2 tablespoons **light
mayonnaise**
1 tablespoon **whole-grain
mustard**
2 tablespoons **all-purpose
flour**
1 **egg**, beaten
salt and **black pepper**

To serve
arugula leaves
lemon wedges

Poach the cod in a saucepan of simmering water for 4–5 minutes, until the fish flakes easily. Remove the fish with a slotted spoon, transfer to a plate, and let cool.

Using a spiralizer fitted with a ⅛ inch spaghetti blade, spiralize the potatoes. Put the spiralized potatoes into a saucepan of boiling water and simmer for 3–4 minutes, until the potatoes are just tender. Drain the potatoes and let them cool slightly.

Flake the fish into a large bowl. Add the potatoes, parsley, mayonnaise, mustard, flour, and egg, mix well, and season with salt and pepper.

Line a large baking sheet with nonstick parchment paper. Place a 3½ inch metal ring or cookie cutter on the baking sheet and fill the ring or cutter with some of the fish mixture to form a thick cake. Remove the ring or cutter and repeat another 7 times to make 8 fish cakes in total.

Bake the fish cakes in a preheated oven, at 400°F, for 20–25 minutes, until crispy. Serve the fish cakes with arugula leaves and lemon wedges to squeeze over them.

For salmon & dill fish cakes, prepare and cook the fish cakes as above, replacing the cod with 8 oz skinless, boneless salmon fillets and the parsley with dill. Serve with wilted spinach.

pork with apple & cider sauce

Serves **2**
Preparation time **5 minutes**
Cooking time **15–18 minutes**

2 **parsnips**, peeled, ends
  trimmed, and halved
  widthwise
1 **red apple**, ends trimmed
1 tablespoon **sunflower oil**
1 tablespoon **butter**
8 oz **pork tenderloin**, cut into
  ½ inch thick slices
scant 1 cup **medium-dry hard
  cider**, **apple cider**, or **apple
  juice**
2 tablespoons chopped **sage**
¼ cup **crème fraîche**
salt and **black pepper**

Using a spiralizer fitted with a ¼ inch flat noodle blade,
spiralize the parsnips and set aside. Change to the
ribbon blade and spiralize the apple. Coarsely snip any
really long ribbons in half with a pair of scissors.

Heat the oil and butter in a large skillet with a lid. Add
the pork and cook over high heat for 2–3 minutes on
each side, until browned. Add the spiralized parsnips and
cook for 2–3 minutes, stirring continuously. Pour over
the hard cider, cider, or apple juice and add the sage and
spiralized apple. Bring to a boil, then reduce the heat to
medium, cover, and simmer for 5–6 minutes, until the
sauce has reduced, the vegetables are just tender, and
the pork is cooked through.

Stir in the crème fraîche and simmer for 2 minutes
or until heated through. Season to taste with salt and
pepper and serve immediately.

For pork with apple & mustard sauce, spiralize
2 parsnips and 1 apple as above. Heat 1 tablespoon
olive oil in a skillet with a lid and cook the sliced pork
as above. Add the spiralized parsnips and cook for
2–3 minutes, stirring continuously. Stir in 2 teaspoons
whole-grain mustard, ⅔ cup sour cream, the spiralized
apple, and a dash of water. Cover and simmer for about
5 minutes, until the vegetables are tender, adding a little
more water if the sauce becomes too thick.

butternut squash & spinach risotto

Serves **2**
Preparation time **10 minutes**
Cooking time **10–12 minutes**

1 small **onion**, ends trimmed
½ small **butternut squash**,
   peeled and halved widthwise
1 tablespoon **olive oil**
1 **garlic clove**, crushed
scant ½ cup **dry white wine**
1 tablespoon chopped **sage**
scant 1 cup hot **vegetable
   broth**
1 (5 oz) package **baby
   spinach**
⅓ cup grated **Parmesan
   cheese**, plus extra to serve
3 oz **goat cheese**, chopped
salt and **black pepper**

To serve
6 crispy fried **sage leaves**
3 tablespoons **pine nuts**,
   toasted

Using a spiralizer fitted with a ⅛ inch spaghetti blade,
spiralize the onion and squash, keeping them separate.

Put the spiralized squash in a food processor and pulse
until it resembles rice.

Heat the oil in a large skillet, add the spiralized onion and
the garlic, and cook over medium heat for 2–3 minutes,
until softened. Pour in the wine and reduce the liquid by
half, then add the squash rice and cook for 2 minutes.
Add the chopped sage and half the broth and cook until
most of the broth has evaporated. Add the remaining
broth, season with salt and pepper, and cook for another
2–3 minutes, until the squash is just tender, adding a little
more hot water, if needed. Add the spinach and vegetarian
pasta cheese or Parmesan and stir for about 2 minutes,
until the spinach has wilted. Stir in the goat cheese and
let melt.

Divide the risotto between 2 plates and serve topped
with crispy sage leaves, toasted pine nuts, and a sprinkling
of Parmesan cheese.

For butternut squash, pancetta & feta risotto,
prepare and cook the risotto as above, omitting the
sage and spinach, replacing the goat cheese with ¾ cup
crumbled feta cheese and 2 tablespoons chopped flat
leaf parsley, and adding 4 oz diced smoked pancetta
to the skillet with the spiralized onion and garlic.
Serve immediately.

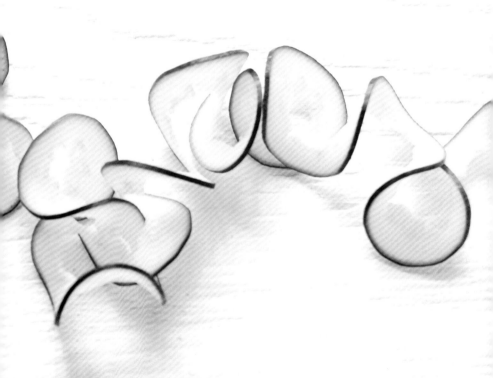

sides

applesauce with apple brandy

Serves **4**
Preparation time **5 minutes**
Cooking time **10 minutes**

3 **crisp apples** (about 1 ½ lb),
  peeled and ends trimmed
finely grated zest of
  ½ **unwaxed lemon**
2 tablespoons **superfine
  sugar**
2 tablespoons **butter**
2 tablespoons **apple brandy**

Using a spiralizer fitted with a ¼ inch flat noodle blade,
spiralize the apples.

Put the spiralized apples into a saucepan with the
remaining ingredients and mix well. Cover and cook over
gentle heat for 8–10 minutes, stirring occasionally, until
the apples are soft. Let the sauce cool.

For spiced applesauce, using a spiralizer fitted with
a ⅛ inch spaghetti blade, spiralize 1 small onion. Melt
2 tablespoonsunsalted butter in a saucepan over low
heat, add the spiralized onion, and cook for 10 minutes
or until softened. Stir in ½ teaspoon ground cinnamon,
a pinch of ground cloves, and a little freshly grated
nutmeg. Meanwhile, spiralize 3 crisp apples using the
flat noodle blade. Stir the spiralized apples into the
onion mixture and add the sugar and lemon zest and
juice. Cover and cook as above. Delicious served with
roast pork.

celeriac remoulade

Serves **4**
Preparation time **10 minutes,
plus standing**

juice of **1 lemon**
generous ¼ cup **light
mayonnaise**
2 tablespoons **reduced-fat
crème fraîche** or **sour
cream**
2 tablespoons **Dijon mustard**
2 tablespoons chopped
parsley
1 **celeriac (celery root)**
salt and **black pepper**

Mix together the lemon juice, mayonnaise, crème fraîche or sour cream, mustard, and parsley in a large bowl and season to taste with salt and pepper.

Using a sharp knife, remove the knobbly parts from the celeriac. Peel the celeriac, cut it in half widthwise, and trim to make the ends flat. Using a spiralizer fitted with a ⅛ inch spaghetti blade, spiralize the celeriac.

Immediately stir the spiralized celeriac into the creamy mixture, until evenly coated, and let stand for 30 minutes before serving.

For roast ham & arugula open sandwiches, cut 2 small French baguettes in half lengthwise, arrange a handful of arugula leaves over the cut side of each baguette half, then top with some slices roast ham and finish with a generous spoonful of celeriac remoulade. Serve immediately.

spicy asian coleslaw

Serves **4–6**
Preparation time **10 minutes**

1 **cucumber**, ends trimmed
   and cut into 3 pieces
   widthwise
1 large **carrot**, peeled, ends
   trimmed, and cut into
   3 pieces widthwise
1 **daikon** (8 oz), peeled,
   ends trimmed, and halved
   widthwise
¼ cup chopped **fresh cilantro**
2 tablespoons **sesame seeds**,
   lightly toasted

For the dressing
finely grated zest and juice of
   2 **unwaxed limes**
1 tablespoon **rice wine
   vinegar**
2 teaspoons grated **fresh
   ginger**
1 small **red chili,** seeded and
   chopped
1 teaspoon packed **light
   brown sugar**
1 teaspoon **sesame oil**

Using a spiralizer fitted with a ⅛ inch spaghetti blade,
spiralize the cucumber and pat dry with paper towels.
Using the same blade, spiralize the carrot and daikon.

To make the dressing, in a small bowl, mix together the
lime zest and juice, vinegar, ginger, chili, sugar, and oil
and stir until the sugar has dissolved.

Put the spiralized cucumber, carrot, and daikon into a
large bowl and sprinkle with the cilantro and sesame
seeds. Pour over the dressing and toss well to coat all
the ingredients. Chill the coleslaw in the refrigerator
until ready to serve.

For kohlrabi & apple slaw, trim both ends of 3 small
kohlrabi. Using a spiralizer fitted with a ¼ inch flat
noodle blade, spiralize the kohlrabi and 2 red apples.
Change to a ⅛ inch spaghetti blade and spiralize
1 red onion. Put the spiralized kohlrabi, apples, and
onion into a large bowl. Whisk together 1 tablespoon
Dijon mustard, 1 tablespoon honey, 1 tablespoon apple
cider vinegar, and ¼ cup extra virgin olive oil, then
season the dressing to taste. Pour the dressing over
the slaw and toss well to coat.

root vegetable hash brown

Serves **4**

Preparation time **10 minutes**

Cooking time **30–40 minutes**

3 **russet potatoes**, peeled
and ends trimmed

2 large **carrots**, peeled,
ends trimmed, and halved
widthwise

1 large **parsnip**, peeled,
ends trimmed, and halved
widthwise

1 **onion**, ends trimmed

1 tablespoon **sunflower oil**

2 teaspoons chopped **thyme
leaves**

salt and **black pepper**

Using a spiralizer fitted with a ⅛ inch spaghetti blade,
spiralize all the potatoes, carrots, parsnip, and onion,
keeping the onion separate.

Put the spiralized potatoes, carrots, and parsnip into a
steamer over a saucepan of boiling water and steam for
5 minutes or until the potatoes are sticky and the carrots
and parsnip are just tender.

Meanwhile, heat the oil in a 9 inch nonstick skillet
and cook the spiralized onion over medium heat for
2–3 minutes, until softened.

Stir in the steamed vegetables and thyme and season
with salt and pepper. Cook for 4–5 minutes, without
stirring, until the bottom of the vegetables starts to crisp.
Turn over the vegetables, pat down, and continue to cook
for another 4–5 minutes. Repeat this process another
2 times or until the hash brown is crispy and cooked
through. Cut into wedges and serve.

For sweet potato hash brown with eggs & spinach,
make the hash brown as above, replacing the carrots
and parsnip with 2 sweet potatoes. Meanwhile,
poach 4 eggs in a saucepan of simmering water for
2–3 minutes, until cooked and the yolks are runny.
Remove the poached eggs with a slotted spoon. Heat
1 tablespoon olive oil in a skillet over medium heat, add
2 cups baby spinach, and cook for 1–2 minutes, until the
spinach has wilted. Serve the hash brown topped with a
poached egg and some wilted spinach.

160

potato fries with rosemary & garlic

Serves **2–3**
Preparation time **5 minutes**
Cooking time **10 minutes**

2 large **russet potatoes**,
  peeled, ends trimmed, and
  halved widthwise
4 cups **vegetable** or
  sunflower oil, for deep frying
4 **rosemary sprigs**
8 **garlic cloves**, unpeeled
sea salt flakes, for sprinkling

Using a spiralizer fitted with a ¼ inch flat noodle blade, spiralize the potatoes.

Heat the oil in a wok or deep, heavy saucepan to 350–375°F or until a cube of bread dropped into the oil turns golden brown in 30 seconds. Alternatively, you can use a deep fryer.

Drop the rosemary and garlic into the hot oil and cook for 1 minute. Add the spiralized potatoes and deep-fry for 6–8 minutes, until golden brown and crispy. Remove from the oil with a slotted spoon and drain on paper towels. Sprinkle the potato fries with sea salt and serve immediately.

For crispy Cajun potato fries, spiralize the potatoes as above. Put the spiralized potatoes into a large bowl, sprinkle with 1 tablespoon Cajun spice mix, and toss well to coat. Deep-fry as above, omitting the rosemary and garlic.

scalloped sweet potatoes

Serves **6**
Preparation time **10 minutes**
Cooking time **1 hour**

1 tablespoon **butter**
4 **white round potatoes**,
    peeled, ends trimmed, and
    halved widthwise
3 **sweet potatoes**, peeled,
    ends trimmed, and halved
    widthwise
1 large **onion**, ends trimmed
2 **garlic cloves**, crushed
2 tablespoons chopped
    rosemary
2 cups **low-fat milk**
1¼ cups **reduced-fat crème
    fraîche** or **sour cream**
salt and **black pepper**

Using a little of the butter, lightly grease a 1½ quart
ovenproof dish. Using a spiralizer fitted with a ribbon
blade, spiralize the potatoes and sweet potatoes,
keeping them separate. Change to a ⅛ inch spaghetti
blade and spiralize the onion.

Melt the remaining butter in a large saucepan over
medium heat. Add the spiralized onion and cook for
3–4 minutes, until softened. Stir in the garlic and
rosemary and cook for 1 minute. Stir in the milk and
crème fraîche or sour cream, season with salt and
pepper, then stir in the spiralized potatoes. Bring to
a simmer, cover, and cook over low heat for 5 minutes.
Stir in the spiralized sweet potatoes, cover, and simmer
for 3 minutes.

Transfer the mixture to the prepared dish, cover with
aluminum foil, and bake in a preheated oven, at 325°F,
for 30 minutes. Remove the foil and cook for another
10 minutes or until the potatoes are tender.

For bacon & cheese scalloped potatoes, prepare the
scalloped sweet potatoes as above, adding 7 oz smoked
bacon pieces to the saucepan with the spiralized onion.
Sprinkle ½ cup shredded sharp cheddar cheese over
the top of the potatoes before baking as above.

baked vegetable chips

Serves **4**

Preparation time **10 minutes**

Cooking time **30–35 minutes**

1 **sweet potato**, peeled, ends trimmed, and halved widthwise

1 large **parsnip**, peeled, ends trimmed, and halved widthwise

2 **fresh beets**, scrubbed and ends trimmed

2 tablespoons **olive oil**

sea salt flakes

Line 2 large baking sheets with nonstick parchment paper.

Using a spiralizer fitted with a ribbon blade, spiralize the sweet potato, parsnip, and beets.

Put the spiralized vegetables into a large bowl, drizzle with the oil, sprinkle with a little sea salt, and mix well.

Spread out the vegetables in a single layer on the prepared baking sheets. Bake in a preheated oven, at 325°F, for 30–35 minutes, turning the vegetables and swapping over the baking sheets in the oven halfway through the cooking time, until the chips are lightly golden and crispy. (Remove any chips that are already golden when you turn over the vegetables.)

Turn off the oven. Return any chips you removed to the baking sheets and let the chips cool in the oven and crisp up—the chips will become extra crispy as they cool. Sprinkle with a little extra sea salt and serve.

For garlic & herb dip, to serve as an accompaniment, mix together ½ cup cream cheese with ¼ cup plain yogurt, then stir in 1 crushed garlic clove and 1 tablespoon freshly chopped chives. Season to taste.

cucumber & mint raita

Serves **4**

Preparation time **5 minutes**

½ **cucumber**, ends trimmed
  and halved widthwise

1 cup **plain yogurt**

2 tablespoons chopped **mint**

½ teaspoon **salt**

½ teaspoon **ground cumin**

Using a spiralizer fitted with a ⅛ inch spaghetti blade, spiralize the cucumber. Dry the spiralized cucumber on paper towels.

Put the cucumber into a large bowl and mix together with all the remaining ingredients. Chill in the refrigerator until ready to serve.

For za'atar tortilla chips, to serve as an accompaniment, brush both sides of 6 flour tortillas with a little sunflower oil, then cut each into 8 triangles with a pair of scissors. Arrange in a single layer on 1 or 2 baking sheets, then sprinkle with a little salt and 1–2 tablespoons zaatar spice mix. Bake in a preheated oven, at 350°F, for 7–8 minutes, until crisp and golden, turning halfway through. Remove from the oven and set aside to cool and continue crisping.

spicy potato curls

Serves **4**
Preparation time **5 minutes**
Cooking time **20 minutes**

4 **russet potatoes**, peeled
  and ends trimmed
2 tablespoons **sunflower oil**
1 teaspoon **garlic salt**
2 teaspoons **smoked paprika**
1 teaspoon **dried mixed**
  herbs
salt and **black pepper**

Line a large baking sheet with parchment paper.

Using a spiralizer fitted with a ¼ inch flat noodle blade, spiralize the potatoes.

Put the spiralized potatoes into a large bowl, add all the remaining ingredients, and mix well to evenly coat the potatoes. Spread out the spiralized potatoes in a single layer on the prepared baking sheet.

Bake in a preheated oven, at 400°F, for 10 minutes, then stir the potato curls, moving the outside crispy ones to the center, and bake for another 10 minutes, until golden and crispy. Serve immediately.

For Parmesan potato curls, prepare and bake the potato curls as above, omitting the smoked paprika. When they have finished baking, remove from the oven, sprinkle with 3 tablespoons finely grated Parmesan cheese, and toss well to coat.

zucchini & cheese chips

Serves **2**
Preparation time **10 minutes**
Cooking time **12–15 minutes**

1 **zucchini**, ends trimmed and halved widthwise
⅓ cup **cornmeal**
½ cup finely grated **Parmesan cheese**
2 **egg whites**
black pepper

Line 2 large baking sheets with parchment paper.

Using a spiralizer fitted with a ribbon blade, spiralize the zucchini. Snip the spirals into 3 inch lengths with a pair of scissors.

Put the cornmeal, Parmesan, and pepper into a bowl and mix together until well combined. In a separate small bowl, whisk the egg whites with a fork until frothy. Place the spiralized zucchini, a few at a time, in the egg whites and turn to coat, then place in the cheese mixture and gently shake until completely coated in the mixture.

Transfer the zucchini to the prepared baking sheets, leaving a small space between each spiral. Sprinkle with any remaining cheese mixture and bake in a preheated oven, at 400°F, for 12–15 minutes, turning once, until crispy. Serve immediately.

For zucchini & tomato gratin, trim the ends and halve widthwise 3 zucchini. Using a spiralizer fitted with a ¼ inch flat noodle blade, spiralize the zucchini. Snip any long strings into smaller pieces with a pair of scissors. Put the spiralized zucchini into a large bowl and toss with 2 tablespoons pesto. Slice 4 tomatoes. Put a layer of zucchini and a layer of tomatoes into a 2 quart ovenproof dish. Repeat the layers until all the zucchini and tomatoes are used. In a small bowl, mix together ¼ cup dried bread crumbs with 1 crushed garlic clove and ⅓ cup finely grated Parmesan cheese. Sprinkle the crumbs over the zucchini and tomatoes, then drizzle with a little olive oil. Bake in a preheated oven, at 400°F, for 25–30 minutes, until the top is golden and vegetables are tender.

moroccan carrot salad

Serves **4**

Preparation time **10 minutes,
plus marinating**

6 large **carrots**, peeled and
halved widthwise

2 tablespoons **orange juice**

1 tablespoon **lemon juice**

2 teaspoons **orange blossom
water**

2 tablespoons **extra virgin
olive oil**

½ teaspoon **ground cumin**

½ teaspoon **ground
cinnamon**

1 teaspoon **confectioners'
sugar**

1 **preserved lemon**, cut in
half, pith and pulp removed,
and skin finely chopped

2 tablespoons chopped **mint**

sea salt flakes and **black
pepper**

handful of **mint leaves**,
to garnish

Using a spiralizer fitted with a ¼ inch flat noodle blade
or a ribbon blade, spiralize the carrots.

Combine the orange and lemon juice, orange blossom
water, oil, cumin, cinnamon, and confectioners' sugar
in a bowl and whisk together. Season to taste with salt
and pepper.

Add the spiralized carrots, preserved lemon, and
mint and lightly toss. Put into the refrigerator and let
marinate for 1–2 hours. Garnish with the mint leaves
just before serving.

For tahini carrot & grain salad, spiralize the carrots as
above. Put the spiralized carrots into a large bowl with
2 cups cooked mixed grains. In a bowl, whisk together
¼ cup tahini, 2 tablespoons lemon juice, 1 tablespoon
olive oil, and 1 teaspoon honey, adding 1–2 tablespoons
cold water if the dressing is too thick. Pour the dressing
over the carrot and grains and toss well to coat.

roasted beet with balsamic glaze

Serves **4**
Preparation time **5 minutes**
Cooking time **15–20 minutes**

4 **fresh beets**, scrubbed and
   ends trimmed
1 tablespoon **olive oil**
3 tablespoons **balsamic
   vinegar**
sea salt flakes and
   black pepper

Using a spiralizer fitted with a ¼ inch flat noodle blade,
spiralize the beets.

Put the spiralized beets into a roasting pan, drizzle with
the oil and 2 tablespoons of the vinegar, and season well
with salt and pepper. Mix well.

Roast the beets in a preheated oven, at 375° F, for
15–20 minutes, turning halfway through the cooking
time, until tender and slightly crispy. Stir in the remaining
vinegar and let cool.

For beets with horseradish cream, spiralize
4 fresh beets as above. Put the spiralized beets into
a large bowl, drizzle with 1 tablespoon olive oil and
1 tablespoon red wine vinegar, and stir well to coat.
Stir in 2 tablespoons crème fraîche or sour cream and
2 teaspoons creamed horseradish sauce and season to
taste. Delicious served with cold roast beef or bresaola.

steamed vegetables with honey

Serves **4**

Preparation time **5 minutes**

Cooking time **5 minutes**

2 large **carrots**, peeled,
   ends trimmed, and halved
   widthwise

3 **zucchini**, ends trimmed and
   halved widthwise

1 tablespoon **honey**

1 tablespoon **lemon juice**

½ teaspoon **caraway seeds**
   (optional)

salt and **black pepper**

Using a spiralizer fitted with a ribbon blade, spiralize the carrots and zucchini.

Mix together the honey, lemon juice, and caraway seeds, if using, in a small bowl.

Put the spiralized carrots into a steamer over a saucepan of boiling water and steam them for 2 minutes. Add the spiralized zucchini and steam for another 3 minutes or until the vegetables are just tender.

Transfer the steamed vegetables to a serving bowl, pour over the honey mixture, and toss well. Season to taste with salt and pepper and serve immediately.

For honey & mustard roasted carrots & parsnips, using a spiralizer fitted with a ribbon blade, spiralize 2 parsnips and 2 carrots. Put the spiralized vegetables into a roasting pan. Mix together 3 tablespoons honey, 1 tablespoon whole-grain mustard, and 1 tablespoon olive oil in a small bowl. Pour over the vegetables and stir gently to coat. Season well. Bake in a preheated oven, at 375°F, for 15–20 minutes, stirring halfway through the cooking time, until tender.

pickles & preserves

easy spiralized vegetable kimchi

Makes **1 (32 oz/1 quart) jar**
Preparation time **15 minutes,
  plus overnight standing
  and fermenting**

1 small head of **napa
  cabbage**, quartered
  lengthwise and cut into
  1 inch strips
2 tablespoons **sea salt**
2 **carrots**, peeled, ends
  trimmed, and halved
  widthwise
½ **daikon**, peeled, ends
  trimmed, and halved
  widthwise
4 **scallions**, chopped

For the kimchi paste
1 inch piece **fresh ginger**,
  peeled and grated
2 **garlic cloves**, crushed
¼ cup **rice vinegar**
1 tablespoon **Thai fish sauce**
2 tablespoons **sriracha chili
  sauce** or **chili paste**
1 teaspoon **superfine sugar**

Put the napa cabbage into a bowl, add the sea salt, and mix together. Let stand for 4–5 hours or overnight.

Using a spiralizer fitted with a ⅛ inch spaghetti blade, spiralize the carrots and daikon.

Put the spiralized vegetables into a large bowl with the scallions. Rinse the napa cabbage under cold running water, drain, and dry thoroughly, then add to the bowl.

To make the kimchi paste, put all the ingredients into a small bowl and blend together. Stir the paste into the vegetables until evenly coated.

Pack the vegetable mixture into a large jar or plastic container, seal, and let ferment at room temperature overnight. Transfer to the refrigerator and use within 2 weeks. The flavor will improve the longer it's left.

For kimchi rice & egg bowls, heat 1 tablespoon sunflower oil in a saucepan over medium heat. Add 6 chopped scallions and ½ seeded and sliced red bell pepper, then cook for 2–3 minutes, until softened. Add 1 tablespoon grated fresh ginger and 1 cup chopped kale, cover with a lid, and cook for 3 minutes or until the kale is just tender. Stir in 1½ cups cooked brown basmati rice and 1 cup Easy Spiralized Vegetable Kimchi (see above) and cook for 2 minutes. Meanwhile, heat 1 tablespoon sunflower oil in a small skillet, crack in 2 eggs, and cook until the whites are set and the yolk is still runny. Divide the kimchi rice between 2 bowls, top each with a fried egg, drizzle with a little sriracha sauce, and garnish with chopped fresh cilantro. Serve immediately.

pickled cucumber & dill spirals

Serves **6–8**

Preparation time **10 minutes, plus 1 day pickling**

1 **cucumber**, ends trimmed and cut into 4 pieces widthwise

⅔ cup **white wine vinegar**

1¼ cups **warm water**

1 teaspoon **superfine sugar**

2 teaspoons **sea salt**

½ cup **dill**, coarsely chopped

4 **garlic cloves**, peeled and smashed

1 teaspoon **black peppercorns**

Using a spiralizer fitted with a ribbon blade, spiralize the cucumber. Dry the spiralized cucumber on paper towels.

Put the vinegar, measured water, sugar, and salt into a nonreactive bowl and whisk together until the sugar and salt have dissolved. Stir in the dill, garlic, and peppercorns.

Put the spiralized cucumber into a 24 oz pickling jar that has a lid. Pour the vinegar mixture over the cucumber and stir well.

Seal the jar and put into the refrigerator for at least 1 day before serving. The pickled cucumber will keep for up to a few weeks in the refrigerator.

For smoked salmon & pickled cucumber & dill sandwiches, in a small bowl, mix together ⅓ cup crème fraîche or sour cream with 1 teaspoon hot horseradish sauce and a squeeze of lemon juice. Spread it over 4 slices of rye bread, then divide 13 oz smoked salmon over the top. Top with drained Pickled Cucumber & Dill Spirals (see above) and serve immediately with plenty of black pepper.

mixed vegetable ribbon pickle

Serves **4**

Preparation time **10 minutes, plus salting and marinating**

1 **carrot**, peeled, ends trimmed, and halved widthwise

1 **cucumber**, ends trimmed and cut into 4 pieces widthwise

1 fresh **golden beet**, scrubbed and ends trimmed

1 cup thinly sliced **radishes**

2 tablespoons **sea salt flakes**

scant 1 cup **white wine vinegar**

⅓ cup **superfine sugar**

scant ½ cup **water**

1 teaspoon **yellow mustard seeds**

2 teaspoons **fennel seeds**

¼ cup coarsely chopped **dill**

Using a spiralizer fitted with a ribbon blade, spiralize the carrot, cucumber, and beet.

Put the spiralized vegetables into a colander standing over a bowl, add the radishes, and sprinkle with the salt. Toss to combine and let stand for 20 minutes. Rinse under cold running water, then drain well.

Put the vinegar, sugar, and measured water into a large jar or nonreactive bowl and stir until the sugar has dissolved. Add the mustard and fennel seeds and dill. Stir in the drained vegetables and seal the jar or cover the bowl. Chill in the refrigerator for at least 20 minutes before serving.

For garlicky vegetable noodle & jalapeno pickle, using a spiralizer fitted with a ⅛ inch spaghetti blade, spiralize 1 carrot, 1 cucumber, and 1 fresh golden beet. Put the spiralized vegetables into a colander standing over a bowl, add 1–2 thinly sliced jalapeño peppers, and sprinkle with 2 tablespoons sea salt flakes. Toss to combine and let stand for 20 minutes. Rinse under cold running water, then drain well. Put scant 1 cup white wine vinegar, scant ½ cup water, and ⅓ cup superfine sugar into a large jar or nonreactive bowl and stir until the sugar has dissolved. Add 2 sliced garlic cloves, 1 teaspoon yellow mustard seeds, 2 teaspoons cumin seeds, and 1 teaspoon dried oregano. Stir in the drained vegetables and seal the jar or cover the bowl. Chill in the refrigerator for at least 20 minutes before serving.

spicy cucumber pickle

Serves **4**

Preparation time **10 minutes, plus marinating**

1 **cucumber**, ends trimmed and cut into 4 pieces widthwise

2 teaspoons **salt**

¼ cup **rice wine vinegar**

3 tablespoons **superfine sugar**

1 small **red chili,** seeded and finely chopped

1 inch piece **fresh ginger,** peeled and grated

Using a spiralizer fitted with a ribbon blade, spiralize the cucumber. Dry the spiralized cucumber on paper towels and put it into a large bowl.

Whisk together all the remaining ingredients in a small bowl and pour the marinade over the cucumber. Gently toss to coat the cucumber, cover, and let marinate for at least 1 hour or overnight in the refrigerator. To serve, drain the pickle from the marinade.

For spicy Korean cucumber pickle, prepare the 1 cucumber as above. In a small bowl, whisk together 2 teaspoons salt, ¼ cup rice wine vinegar, 3 tablespoons superfine sugar, 1–2 teaspoons gochujang (Korean chili paste), and 1 teaspoon sesame seeds. Pour the marinade over the cucumber and let marinate for 1 hour in the refrigerator. Use and store as above.

butternut squash marmalade

Makes **4 (8–9 oz) jars**
Preparation time **15 minutes**
Cooking time **about 1 hour**

1 large or 2 medium **butternut squash** (the nonbulbous ends), peeled and halved widthwise
2 **unwaxed oranges**, thinly sliced and halved
juice of 2 **lemons**
¾ cup peeled and thinly sliced **fresh ginger** (optional)
2½ cups **water**
4 cups **granulated sugar**

Using a spiralizer fitted with a ⅛ inch spaghetti blade, spiralize the squash.

Put the spiralized squash into a preserving pan or wide saucepan, add the oranges, lemon juice, and ginger, if using, and pour over the water. Bring to a boil, then reduce the heat and simmer for 20–25 minutes, until the oranges are tender.

Add the sugar and cook over low heat, stirring, until it has dissolved. Increase the heat to high and bring to a boil, then reduce the heat to medium and simmer for 25–30 minutes, until the mixture is thick and syrupy and leaves a clear channel when a wooden spoon is drawn through it.

Let the marmalade cool in the pan for 5 minutes, then carefully ladle into hot sterilized jars and seal.

For spiced butternut squash marmalade, prepare and cook the marmalade as above, adding 1 teaspoon ground cinnamon and a pinch of ground nutmeg to the marmalade mixture when you add the fresh ginger.

quick apple & ginger preserves

Serves **4**

Preparation time **5 minutes**

Cooking time **10–15 minutes**

2 **Granny Smith apples**,
  peeled and ends trimmed

¼ cup **superfine sugar**, or
  to taste

2 inch piece **fresh ginger**,
  peeled and grated

1 tablespoon **lemon juice**

Using a spiralizer fitted with a ¼ inch flat noodle blade, spiralize the apples.

Put the spiralized apples into a saucepan with the sugar and ginger. Cook over medium heat, stirring gently, until the sugar has dissolved. Bring to a boil, then reduce the heat and simmer for 8–10 minutes, until the apples are tender.

Stir in the lemon juice and cook for another 2–3 minutes, until the preserves have thickened and reduced. Let cool before serving. The preserves will keep for up to 2–3 days in the refrigerator.

For quick pear & vanilla preserves, peel and trim the pointy ends of 4 large, firm pears. Using the flat noodle blade, spiralize the pears. Put the spiralized pears into a saucepan. Cut 1 vanilla bean in half lengthwise, scrape out the seeds, and add them to the pears with ¼ cup superfine sugar. Cook over medium heat, stirring until the sugar dissolves. Bring to a boil, then reduce the heat and simmer for 8–10 minutes, until the pears are tender. Stir in 1 tablespoon lemon juice and cook for another 2 minutes or until the preserves have thickened and reduced. Cool and store as above.

zucchini & ginger preserves

Makes about **4 (14½ oz) jars**
Preparation time **5 minutes**
Cooking time **20–25 minutes**

5 **zucchini** (about 2 lb),
   ends trimmed and halved
   widthwise
¾ cup peeled and grated
   fresh ginger
finely grated zest and juice of
   2 **unwaxed lemons**
5 cups **gelling sugar**
   (available online, sometimes
   labeled as jam sugar)

Using a spiralizer fitted with a ⅛ inch spaghetti blade, spiralize the zucchini. Coarsely snip any really long strands in half with a pair of scissors.

Put the spiralized zucchini into a preserving pan or wide saucepan with the ginger and lemon zest and juice. Cook over low heat, stirring occasionally, for 3–4 minutes, until the zucchini start to release their liquid.

Add the sugar and cook gently, stirring until it has dissolved. Increase the heat to high and bring to a boil. Boil for 15–20 minutes, until reduced and glossy. To test whether the preserves have set, place a little on a cold saucer and let stand for a few minutes. Gently push the preserves with your finger—if there are wrinkles, the preserves have reached setting point.

Remove from the heat and spoon off any foam from the surface. Let the preserves cool in the pan for 10 minutes, then carefully pour into hot sterilized jars and seal. The preserves will keep for a few weeks or process in a hot water bath for longer storage.

For feta bruschetta with zucchini & ginger preserves, toast 4 slices of ciabatta under a preheated hot broiler. Top each slice with a handful of baby spinach, then divide 1 cup crumbled feta among them. Top with a large spoonful of the Zucchini & Ginger Preserves (see above) and serve immediately.

baking &
sweet treats

butternut squash & chili cornbread

Makes **1 loaf**
Preparation time **10 minutes**
Cooking time **25–30 minutes**

2 tablespoons **coconut oil** or
   melted butter, plus extra for
   greasing
¼ **butternut squash** (the
   nonbulbous end), peeled
   and halved widthwise
1 cup **all-purpose flour**
1 cup **cornmeal**
2 teaspoons **baking powder**
1 teaspoon **salt**
4 **scallions**, thinly chopped
1 **red chili,** seeded and finely
   chopped
2 **eggs**
1 cup **buttermilk**

Grease an 8 inch springform cake pan and line the
bottom with nonstick parchment paper.

Using a spiralizer fitted with a ⅛ inch spaghetti blade,
spiralize the squash. Coarsely snip any really long spirals
in half with a pair of scissors.

Mix together the flour, cornmeal, baking powder, salt,
scallions, chili, and spiralized squash in a large bowl.

Whisk together the eggs, buttermilk, and oil or melted
butter in a small bowl, then pour the wet ingredients
over the dry ingredients. Mix well until all the ingredients
are combined.

Pour the batter into the prepared pan and bake in a
preheated oven, at 400°F, for 25–30 minutes, until
golden brown, firm, and beginning to pull away from the
sides of the pan. Remove from the oven and let cool
slightly in the pan.

Serve warm, sliced, or cut into wedges.

For individual cornbreads, line a 12-cup muffin pan
with muffin liners. Prepare the cornbread batter as
above and divide it among the muffin liners. Bake in a
preheated oven, at 400°F, for about 20 minutes, until
golden brown, risen, and firm.

zucchini & cheese soda bread

Makes **1 medium loaf**
Preparation time **10 minutes**
Cooking time **25–30 minutes**

1 large **zucchini**, ends trimmed
  and halved widthwise
1¾ cups **whole-wheat flour**
1¾ cups **all-purpose flour**,
  plus extra for dusting
½ teaspoon **sea salt**
1 teaspoon **superfine sugar**
1 teaspoon **baking soda**
⅔ cup shredded **sharp
  cheddar cheese**
1½–1⅔ cups **buttermilk**, plus
  extra for brushing

Using a spiralizer fitted with a ⅛ inch spaghetti blade,
spiralize the zucchini. Put the zucchini onto a clean
dish towel or paper towels and gently squeeze out any
excess liquid.

Put a large casserole dish and its lid into a preheated
oven, at 425°F.

Using your hands, mix together the spiralized zucchini,
flours, salt, sugar, baking soda, and ½ cup of the cheese in
a large bowl. Stir in enough of the buttermilk to bring the
mixture together to make a soft dough.

Transfer the dough onto a lightly floured surface and
knead lightly, then shape into a shallow, round loaf about
1½ inches thick. Make a cross in the top, brush with a
little buttermilk, and sprinkle with the remaining cheese.

Carefully remove the hot casserole dish from the oven
and dust the inside lightly with flour. Gently lower in the
dough, cover with the lid, and return to the oven. Bake
for 25–30 minutes, until the loaf is golden and sounds
hollow when tapped.

Let the bread cool in the dish for 5 minutes, then remove
from the dish and transfer to a cooling rack to cool
slightly before serving.

For apple & cheese soda bread, make the bread as
above, replacing the zucchini with 2 apples; you can
also substitute the cheddar cheese for another type,
such as Colby or Monterey Jack cheese.

apple & blackberry crumb muffins

Makes **10**
Preparation time **10 minutes**
Cooking time **20–25 minutes**

2 **red crisp apples**, ends
  trimmed
2½ cups **all-purpose flour**
1 tablespoon **baking powder**
½ teaspoon **salt**
1 teaspoon **ground cinnamon**
⅔ cup **superfine sugar**
1 extra-large **egg**
1 cup **milk**
⅓ cup **sunflower oil**
1 cup **blackberries**

For the topping
3½ tablespoons **all-purpose
  flour**
1 tablespoon **cold butter**
2 tablespoons **Demerara
  sugar**

Line a muffin pan with 10 paper muffin liners.

To make the topping, put the flour into a small bowl, add the butter, and rub in with your fingertips until the mixture resembles fine bread crumbs. Stir in the sugar and set aside.

Using a spiralizer fitted with a ¼ inch flat noodle blade, spiralize the apples.

Sift together the flour, baking powder, and salt in a large bowl, then stir in the cinnamon and sugar. In a small bowl, beat together the egg, milk, and oil, then pour the wet ingredients over the dry ingredients. Mix until just combined, then stir in the spiralized apples and the blackberries. Divide the batter among the muffin liners and sprinkle the tops with the crumb topping. Bake in a preheated oven, at 375°F, for 20–25 minutes, until risen and firm.

For apple, golden raisin & cinnamon muffins, prepare the muffins as above, replacing the blackberries with 1 cup golden raisins. Replace the crumb topping 2 tablespoons light brown sugar mixed with ½ teaspoon ground cinnamon and bake as above.

beet & vanilla cupcakes

Makes **18**
Preparation time **15 minutes,
plus cooling**
Cooking time **18–20 minutes**

2 **fresh beets**, scrubbed and
ends trimmed
1½ sticks (6 oz) **unsalted
butter**, softened
¾ cup plus 2 tablespoons
superfine sugar
2 extra-large **eggs**, beaten
1 tablespoon **vanilla extract**
1½ cups **all-purpose flour**
1½ teaspoons **baking powder**

For the frosting
¾ cup **light cream cheese**
2 tablespoons **confectioners'
sugar**, sifted
1 tablespoon **vanilla extract**

Line 1 or 2 cupcake pans with 18 paper cupcake liners.

Using a spiralizer fitted with a ⅛ inch spaghetti
blade, spiralize the beets. Reserving a few spirals for
decoration, put the remaining spiralized beets into a food
processor and pulse until they resemble rice.

Beat together the butter and sugar in a large bowl until
light and fluffy. Whisk in the eggs, a little at a time, then
whisk in the vanilla extract. Sift in the flour and baking
powder and stir until just combined, then fold in the
beet rice.

Divide the batter between the cupcake liners. Bake in a
preheated oven, at 350°F, for 18–20 minutes, until risen
and golden brown. Remove from the oven, transfer to a
cooling rack, and let cool completely.

To make the frosting, put all the frosting ingredients
into a bowl and beat together until smooth. Spread the
frosting over the cooled cupcakes and decorate with the
reserved beet spirals.

For red velvet cupcakes, prepare and bake the
cupcakes as above, replacing ¼ cup of the flour with
¼ cup unsweetened cocoa powder. Decorate the cakes
as above, adding some red sprinkles.

apple frangipane tart

Serves **8**
Preparation time **15 minutes**
Cooking time **1 hour**

1 (9 inch) **rolled dough pie
crust** or **prepared pie
dough** (enough for one
9 inch pie crust)
6 tablespoons **unsalted
butter**
½ cup **superfine sugar**
2 large **eggs**
2 cups **almond meal**
½ teaspoon **almond extract**
1 tablespoon **all-purpose
flour**, plus extra for dusting
2 **red crisp apples**, ends
trimmed
¼ cup **slivered almonds**
2 tablespoons **apricot
preserves** or **jam**
whipped or **heavy cream**,
to serve

Roll out the dough on a lightly floured surface until large enough to fit a 9 inch loose-bottom tart pan. Line the pan with the dough. Prick the bottom with a fork, cover with nonstick parchment paper, and fill with pie weights or dried beans. Put the pan onto a baking sheet and bake in a preheated oven, at 375°F, for about 15 minutes. Remove the weights and paper and return to the oven for 5 minutes or until golden.

In a large bowl, cream together the butter and sugar until light and fluffy. Gradually beat in the eggs, then stir in the ground almonds, almond extract, and flour. Spoon the filling into the pastry shell.

Using a spiralizer fitted with a ¼ inch flat noodle blade, spiralize the apples.

Arrange the spiralized apples on top of the tart and sprinkle with the slivered almonds. Bake in a preheated oven, at 350°F, for 40–45 minutes, until golden and set.

Warm the apricot preserves or jam in a small saucepan, then brush it over the top of the tart. Serve slices of the tart with spoonfuls of whipped or heavy cream.

For apple brandy cream to serve with the tart, lightly whip together 2½ cups heavy cream and 2 tablespoons confectioners' sugar in a bowl until soft peaks start to form. Add ¼ cup apple brandy and whip until just holding its shape. Chill until ready to serve.

asian pear fruit salad

Serves **4**

Preparation time **5 minutes,
plus cooling**

Cooking time **10 minutes**

½ cup **superfine sugar**

2 **lemon grass stalks**, bruised
and coarsely chopped

1 inch piece **fresh ginger**,
peeled and finely sliced

⅔ cup **cold water**

4 firm **Asian pears** (you can
use normal pears or apples
if you can't find Asian pears),
ends trimmed

2 tablespoons chopped **mint**

½ cup **pomegranate seeds**

¼ cup **fresh** or **dried coconut
shavings** or **coconut flakes**

Put the sugar, lemon grass, ginger, and measured
water into a saucepan. Cook over low heat, stirring
occasionally, until the sugar has dissolved. Bring the
syrup to a boil, then reduce the heat and simmer for
5 minutes. Remove from heat and let cool.

When the syrup has cooled, use a spiralizer fitted with
a ribbon blade to spiralize the pears—don't do this ahead
of time or the pears will brown. Put the spiralized pears
into a salad bowl.

Remove the lemon grass from the syrup and discard.
Pour the syrup over the pears, then gently stir in the mint
and pomegranate seeds. Chill in the refrigerator until
ready to serve. To serve, divide the salad among 4 bowls
and sprinkle with the coconut.

For autumnal fruit salad, in a large bowl, whisk
together 3 tablespoons maple syrup with ½ teaspoon
vanilla extract, 1 teaspoon finely grated lemon zest,
2 tablespoons lemon juice, and ¼ teaspoon ground
cinnamon. Using a spiralizer fitted with a ribbon blade,
spiralize 2 firm pears and 2 red crisp apples. Add
the spiralized fruit to the bowl with the syrup. Stir in
1¾ cups fresh blackberries and chill in the refrigerator
to let the flavors develop.

orange, carrot & almond cake

Serves **8–10**

Preparation time **20 minutes, plus cooling**

Cooking time **about 2½ hours**

2 **unwaxed oranges**

butter, for greasing

2 **carrots**, peeled, ends trimmed, and halved widthwise

4 **eggs**

1½ cups **superfine sugar**

3 cups **almond meal**

1 teaspoon **baking powder**

4 **cardamom pods**, seeds crushed

For the syrup

grated zest and juice of
  1 **unwaxed orange**

½ cup **superfine sugar**

2 tablespoons **water**

1 teaspoon **orange blossom water**

Put the oranges into a large saucepan and pour over enough boiling water to cover. Simmer, covered, for 1 hour or until tender. Drain and let cool.

Grease an 8 inch springform cake pan and line the bottom with nonstick parchment paper. Using a spiralizer fitted with a ⅛ inch spaghetti blade, spiralize the carrots. Coarsely snip any really long spirals in half with a pair of scissors.

Cut the cooled oranges in half and remove any seeds. Put into a food processor and process until smooth.

Whisk together the eggs and sugar with a handheld electric mixer in a large mixing bowl, until thick and pale. Gently fold in the processed oranges, spiralized carrots, reserving a few spirals for decoration, the ground almonds, baking powder, and cardamom until combined.

Spoon the batter into the prepared pan and bake in the center of a preheated oven, at 325°F, for 1–1¼ hours or until a toothpick inserted in the center comes out clean. Cover the top with aluminum foil if it becomes too brown during cooking. Remove from the oven and let the cake cool completely in the pan.

To make the syrup, put the orange juice, sugar, and measured water into a saucepan. Cook over low heat, stirring, for 5 minutes or until the sugar has dissolved and the syrup has thickened slightly. Remove from the heat, stir in the orange blossom water, orange zest, and reserved carrot spirals, and let cool.

Remove the cake from the pan and drizzle with the syrup.

pear tarte tatin

Serves **4–6**
Preparation time **10 minutes**
Cooking time **40 minutes**

3 large firm **pears**, pointy ends
   trimmed
⅔ cup **superfine sugar**
3 tablespoons **cold butter**,
   cubed
½ teaspoon **ground ginger**
flour, for dusting
1 (12 oz) sheet **ready-to-bake
   puff pastry**, thawed if frozen
heavy cream, to serve

Using a spiralizer fitted with a ¼ inch flat noodle blade,
spiralize the pears.

Put an 8½ inch ovenproof skillet over medium heat. Add
the sugar and heat for 4–5 minutes, stirring constantly,
until the sugar is a caramel color. Add the butter and
ginger and stir to combine.

Put the spiralized pears into the caramel and spoon
over the mixture until the pears are coated. Reduce the
heat and cook for 4–5 minutes, until slightly softened.
Remove from the heat and let cool slightly.

Roll out the dough on a lightly floured surface to about
¼ inch thick. Cut a disk slightly larger than your skillet
(about 9½ inches in diameter). Put the dough disk on
top of the pears, then carefully tuck it snugly around the
outside of the pears and down into the sides of the pan.

Bake the tart in a preheated oven, at 400°F, for
30 minutes or until the pastry is golden brown and
puffed up. Remove from the oven and let stand for
10 minutes.

Loosen the edges with a knife, place a large serving
plate over the top, and carefully invert the pan to turn the
tart onto the plate. Serve with heavy cream.

For boozy ginger cream, to serve with the tart,
put 1¼ cups heavy cream into a large bowl with
2 tablespoons pear liqueur or rum, 2 tablespoons
confectioners' sugar, and 1 teaspoon ground ginger.
Beat with an electric handheld mixer until the mixture
forms soft peaks.

sweet potato & choc chip cookies

Makes **about 15**
Preparation time **10 minutes**
Cooking time **10–12 minutes**

1 large **sweet potato** (about
    8 oz), peeled, ends trimmed,
    and halved widthwise
½ cup **rolled oats**
½ teaspoon **ground
    cinnamon** or **allspice**
⅓ cup **semisweet chocolate
    chips**
2 **eggs**, beaten
3 tablespoons **almond butter**
1 tablespoon **honey**
1 teaspoon **vanilla extract**

Line 2 large baking sheets with parchment paper.

Using a spiralizer fitted with a ⅛ inch spaghetti blade, spiralize the sweet potato. Put the spiralized sweet potato into a food processor and pulse until it resembles rice.

Put the sweet potato rice into a bowl with the oats, cinnamon or allspice, and chocolate chips and stir to combine.

Beat together the eggs, almond butter, honey, and vanilla extract in a small bowl. Add the sweet potato mixture and mix together.

Drop heaping tablespoonfuls of the dough onto the prepared baking sheets and flatten slightly. Bake in a preheated oven, at 350°F, for 10–12 minutes, until lightly golden.

Remove from the oven and let the cookies cool on the sheets for 5 minutes, then transfer to a cooling rack to cool completely. The cookies will keep for up to 2 days in an airtight container.

For sweet potato & peanut butter cookies, prepare and bake the cookies as above, reducing the quantity of chocolate chips to ¼ cup, adding 3 tablespoons chopped peanuts with the chocolate chips, and replacing the almond butter with 3 tablespoons crunchy peanut butter.

apple, raspberry & almond crisps

Serves **4**
Preparation time **10 minutes**
Cooking time **20–25 minutes**

2 large or 3 medium **red crisp apples**, ends trimmed
1⅔ cups **fresh raspberries**
2 tablespoons **superfine sugar**
¼ cup **apple juice**
custard or **vanilla ice cream**, to serve

For the topping
1 cup **all-purpose flour**
6 tablespoons **butter**
¼ cup **superfine sugar**
¼ cup **almond meal**

Using a spiralizer fitted with a ¼ inch flat noodle blade, spiralize the apples.

Put the spiralized apples into a large bowl and gently mix together with the raspberries and sugar. Divide the mixture among 4 (1 cup) ovenproof dishes and spoon 1 tablespoon of apple juice over the mixture in each dish.

Next, make the topping. In a large bowl, rub together the flour with the butter until the mixture resembles fine bread crumbs (or use a food processor to do this). Stir in the sugar and almonds.

Sprinkle the topping over the apple and raspberry mixture, dividing the topping among the 4 dishes. Bake in a preheated oven, at 375°F, for 20–25 minutes, until golden and bubbling. Serve with custard or vanilla ice cream.

For apple & blackberry oat bar crisps, prepare the filling as above, replacing the raspberries with 1⅓ cups fresh blackberries. To make the topping, put ⅓ cup light corn syrup, ⅓ cup Demerara sugar, and 6 tablespoons butter into a saucepan over medium heat, stirring until the sugar has dissolved. Remove from the heat and stir in 1⅓ cups rolled oats and ¼ cup all-purpose flour. Spoon the topping over the apple and blackberry mixture and bake as above.

carrot cake muffins

Makes **12**
Preparation time **10 minutes**
Cooking time **18–20 minutes**

2 large **carrots**, peeled,
 ends trimmed, and halved
 widthwise
1½ sticks (6 oz) **unsalted
 butter**, softened
¾ cup plus 2 tablespoons
 superfine sugar
grated zest of 1 **unwaxed
 orange** and 1 tablespoon
 orange juice
1⅓ cups **all-purpose flour**
1½ teaspoons **baking powder**
2 teaspoons **ground allspice**
2 extra-large **eggs**
½ cup chopped **walnuts**

For the frosting
¾ cup **low-fat cream cheese**
2 tablespoons **confectioners'
 sugar**
1 tablespoon **orange juice**
2 teaspoons grated **orange
 zest**

Line a muffin pan with 12 paper muffin liners.

Using a spiralizer fitted with a ⅛ inch spaghetti blade,
spiralize the carrots.

Beat together the butter, sugar, and orange zest in
large bowl until pale and fluffy. Sift over the flour, baking
powder, and allspice, then add the eggs and orange juice
and whisk together until well combined. Stir in three-
quarters of the spiralized carrots and the walnuts.

Divide the batter among the muffin liners. Bake in
a preheated oven, at 350°F, for 18–20 minutes, until
risen and golden brown. Remove from the oven, place
on a cooling rack, and let cool.

To make the frosting, beat together all the ingredients
in a bowl until smooth. Spoon the frosting into a pastry
bag fitted with a star-shaped tip and pipe the frosting
onto the cooled muffins. Decorate the muffins with the
remaining carrot curls.

For carrot, golden raisin & cinnamon muffins,
prepare 10 muffin liners and spiralize 2 carrots as
above. In a bowl, sift together 2¼ cups all-purpose
flour, 1 tablespoon baking powder, and ½ teaspoon
salt. Stir in 1 teaspoon ground cinnamon and ⅔ cup
superfine sugar. In a small bowl, beat together 1 extra-
large egg, ⅔ cup milk, and ⅓ cup sunflower oil. Pour
the egg mixture over the flour mixture and stir until
just combined. Stir in the spiralized carrots, ⅓ cup
golden raisins, and ½ cup chopped pecans. Divide the
batter among the liners, then sprinkle the tops with
2 tablespoons light brown sugar. Bake in a preheated
oven, at 375°F, for 20–25 minutes, until risen and firm.

apple carpaccio with mint sugar

Serves **4–6**
Preparation time **10 minutes**

4 **red** or **pink crisp apples**,
  ends trimmed
grated zest and juice of
  1 unwaxed lime
2 tablespoons **superfine
  sugar**
2 heaping tablespoons **mint
  leaves**

Using a spiralizer fitted with a ribbon blade, spiralize the apples. Arrange over a large platter and squeeze the lime juice over them.

Put the sugar, lime zest, and mint into a food processor and process to make a bright green sugar. Sprinkle it over the apples and serve immediately.

For apple carpaccio with lime & chili syrup, put 1 seeded and thinly sliced red chili, the grated zest and juice of 1 unwaxed lime, ⅔ cup superfine sugar, and ⅔ cup cold water into a saucepan, then stir over low heat until the sugar has dissolved. Bring to a boil, then reduce the heat and simmer for 8 minutes, until syrupy. Let cool slightly. Spiralize the apples as above, then put them into a large bowl and pour over the warm syrup.

candied lemon peel

Makes **enough to decorate 2 large cakes**
Preparation time **5 minutes, plus cooling**
Cooking time **10 minutes**

4 large **unwaxed lemons**
½ cup **superfine sugar**, plus about 2 tablespoons superfine sugar for sprinkling
scant ½ cup **cold water**

Cut the lemons in half widthwise and squeeze out the juice. (The juice isn't needed for this recipe, so store it in the refrigerator to be used another time.) Secure the uncut end of one of the lemon halves to a spiralizer fitted with a ribbon blade and spiralize into strips. Repeat with the remaining lemon halves. Remove any of the pith that has separated from the lemon peel.

Put the superfine sugar and measured water into a small saucepan and bring to a boil, stirring continuously. Add the spiralized lemon peel and boil for 4–5 minutes, until syrupy and the peel is translucent.

Line a baking sheet with nonstick parchment paper. Spread out the peel in a single layer on the prepared baking sheet and separate the lemon peel spirals with a fork. Sprinkle with the remaining sugar, then roll the peel in the sugar to coat thoroughly.

Let the peel dry in a warm place for a couple of hours or overnight, if possible. The candied peel can be stored for up to 3 weeks in an airtight container.

For lavender-infused candied lemon peel, prepare and cook the lemon peel as above, replacing the superfine sugar with lavender sugar. The candied peel can be used as a decoration for cakes or a lemon tart or lemon meringue pie.

steamed carrot & ginger cakes

Serves **4**

Preparation time **10 minutes**

Cooking time **30–35 minutes**

1 large **carrot**, peeled, ends trimmed, and halved widthwise

1 stick (4 oz) **butter**, softened, plus extra for greasing

¼ cup **preserved ginger syrup**, plus extra to serve

⅔ cup **superfine sugar**

2 **eggs**, beaten

1 cup **all-purpose flour**

1 teaspoon **baking powder**

2 tablespoons **milk**

4 pieces **preserved ginger**, finely chopped

custard or **cream**, to serve

Using a spiralizer fitted with a ⅛ inch spaghetti blade, spiralize the carrot. Coarsely snip any long spirals into shorter lengths with a pair of scissors.

Grease 4 (⅔ cup) individual metal pans, then spoon 1 tablespoon ginger syrup into the bottom of each pan.

Beat together the butter and sugar in a large bowl until light and fluffy. Gradually beat in the eggs. Gently fold in the flour, baking powder, milk, preserved ginger, and spiralized carrot.

Divide the batter among the prepared pans, then cover each pan tightly with aluminum foil and put into a roasting pan. Pour enough boiling water into the pan to come ¾ inch up the sides of the pans. Bake in a preheated oven, at 350°F, for 30–35 minutes, until a toothpick inserted in the center comes out clean.

Let the steamed cakes cool in the pans for 5 minutes, then run a knife around the inside of the pans to loosen. Turn out onto plates and drizzle with extra ginger syrup. Serve immediately with custard or cream.

For homemade quick creamy custard, put a 12 oz can evaporated milk in a saucepan with 2 tablespoons superfine sugar and 1 teaspoon vanilla extract. In a small bowl, blend 2 tablespoons custard powder with ¼ cup cold water to form a paste. Add the custard paste to the evaporated milk mixture and cook over low heat, whisking continuously, until the custard has boiled and thickened.

baked pears with salted caramel

Serves **4**

Preparation time **15 minutes**

Cooking time **35–40 minutes**

4 firm **Conference pears**, pointy ends trimmed

1 cup **all-purpose flour**

2 teaspoons **baking powder**

⅔ cup **superfine sugar**

scant 1 cup **milk**

7 tablespoons **butter**, melted, plus extra for greasing

1 **egg**, beaten

¾ cup packed **light brown sugar**

¼ cup **light corn syrup**

2 teaspoon **sea salt flakes**

1 cup **water**

vanilla ice cream, to serve

Grease a 1 ½ quart ovenproof dish.

Using a spiralizer fitted with a ¼ inch flat noodle blade, spiralize the pears. Put the spiralized pears into the bottom of the prepared dish.

Sift the flour and baking powder into a large bowl. Add the superfine sugar, milk, melted butter, and egg and whisk together for 2–3 minutes, until well combined. Pour the mixture over the pears.

To make the salted caramel sauce, put the brown sugar, light corn syrup, and salt into a small saucepan and add the measured water. Cook over a moderate heat, stirring, until the sugar has dissolved, then bring to a boil.

Carefully pour the sauce over the dessert and bake in a preheated oven, at 350°F, for 30–35 minutes, until the sponge is set. Let the dessert to stand for 5 minutes before serving with vanilla ice cream.

For vanilla poached pears with warm fudge

sauce, put ¼ cup superfine sugar, 1 vanilla bean split lengthwise, 1 tablespoon lemon juice, and 2½ cups cold water into a large saucepan. Bring to a boil, stirring, until the sugar had dissolved, then simmer for 10 minutes, until reduced by half. Spiralize the pears using a ribbon blade, then add to the syrup and simmer for 2–3 minutes, until softened. To make the fudge sauce, put 6 tablespoons butter, ¾ cup packed light brown sugar, 1 (5 oz) can evaporated milk, and 1 tablespoon light corn syrup into a saucepan and bring to a boil. Simmer for 3–4 minutes, until thickened. Drain the pears from the syrup and serve with the fudge sauce.

cucumber, lemon & mint ice pops

Makes **8**
Preparation time **10 minutes,**
   plus cooling and freezing
Cooking time **5 minutes**

water
juice of 2 large **lemons**
¼ cup **superfine sugar**
10 **mint leaves**, finely
   chopped
½ **cucumber**, ends trimmed
   and halved widthwise

Put the measured water, lemon juice, and sugar into a saucepan. Cook over low heat, stirring, until the sugar has dissolved. Pour into a small bowl and let cool, then stir in the mint.

Using a spiralizer fitted with a ⅛ inch spaghetti blade, spiralize the cucumber.

Divide the spiralized cucumber between 8 ice pop molds, then pour in the lemon and mint mixture to come nearly to the top of the molds. Add an ice pop stick to each mold and freeze for 3–4 hours or until frozen.

For strawberry & mint ice pops with Pimm's, put 3 cups halved and hulled strawberries and 10 mint leaves into a blender and process until smooth. Strain the strawberry mixture through a strainer set over a bowl to remove the seeds. Add ⅓ cup Pimm's (or 2 tablespoons each of gin and red vermouth and 1 tablespoon curaçao), 1 cup lemon-flavored soda, and ½ cup superfine sugar to the strawberry and mint mixture, stirring together until combined and the sugar is dissolved. Spiralize ½ cucumber as above. Divide the spiralized cucumber among 8 ice pop molds, then pour in the strawberry and mint mixture to come nearly to the top of the molds. Add a ice pop stick to each mold and freeze for 3–4 hours, until frozen.

zucchini & lemon drizzle cake

Serves **8**
Preparation time **20 minutes**
Cooking time **40–45 minutes**

2 **zucchini**, ends trimmed and
   halved widthwise
finely grated zest of
   2 **unwaxed lemons**
1¾ sticks (7 oz) **unsalted**
   butter, softened, plus extra
   for greasing
1 cup **superfine sugar**
3 **eggs**, beaten
1⅔ cups **all-purpose flour**,
   sifted
1¾ teaspoons **baking powder**
a small handful of **Candied**
   Lemon Peel (see page 222),
   to decorate

For the lemon syrup
⅓ cup **granulated sugar**
juice of 2 **lemons** (scant
   ½ cup)

Grease an 8 inch springform cake pan and line the bottom with nonstick parchment paper.

Using a spiralizer fitted with a ⅛ inch spaghetti blade, spiralize the zucchini. Coarsely snip any really long spirals in half with a pair of scissors.

Put the lemon zest, butter, and sugar into a mixing bowl and beat until light and fluffy. Add the eggs a little at a time, whisking well after each addition. If the mixture starts to curdle, add 1 tablespoon of the flour. Using a metal spoon, fold in the spiralized zucchini and flour until you have a really thick batter.

Spoon the batter into the prepared pan and bake in the center of a preheated oven, at 350°F, for 40–45 minutes, until risen and golden.

Meanwhile, as soon as the cake is in the oven, make the lemon syrup. Put the sugar and lemon juice into a small bowl and let stand in a warm place, stirring occasionally.

Remove the cake from the oven and prick all over the surface with a toothpick. Slowly drizzle with the lemon syrup, waiting a few moments for it to sink in before adding more. Let the cake cool for 10 minutes, then remove from the pan and transfer to a cooling rack. Decorate with the candied lemon peel.

For zucchini and lime drizzle cake, prepare and bake the cake as above, replacing the lemon zest with the finely grated zest of 2 unwaxed limes and replacing the lemon juice for the syrup with scant ½ cup lime juice.

spiralized apple puff pastry tart

Serves **6–8**
Preparation time **10 minutes**
Cooking time **15–20 minutes**

1 sheet (10½ oz) **ready-to-
    bake puff pastry**, thawed
    if frozen
2 **red** or **green crisp apples**,
    ends trimmed
juice of **1 lemon**
4 tablespoons **butter**, diced
3 tablespoons **superfine
    sugar**
¼ cup **apricot preserves**
vanilla ice cream, to serve

Unroll the pastry dough and place on a nonstick baking sheet. Using a sharp knife, score a 1 inch border around the edges, being careful not to cut all the way through the dough.

Using a spiralizer fitted with a ribbon blade, spiralize the apples. Put the spiralized apples into a bowl and toss in the lemon juice.

Dot some of the butter over the dough and sprinkle with 1 tablespoon of the sugar. Arrange the apples over the dough, then dot with the remaining butter and sprinkle with the remaining sugar.

Bake in a preheated oven, at 425°F, for 15–20 minutes, until risen, golden, and crisp.

Warm the apricot preserves in a small saucepan, then brush over the apples and pastry. Serve immediately with scoops of vanilla ice cream.

For speedy apple compote, to be served as an accompaniment, using a spiralizer fitted with a ¼ inch flat noodle blade, spiralize 4 crisp apples. Melt 4 tablespoons butter in a saucepan, then add the spiralized apples, 2 tablespoons superfine sugar, and ½ teaspoon ground cinnamon. Cook for 4–5 minutes, stirring occasionally, until the apples have softened.

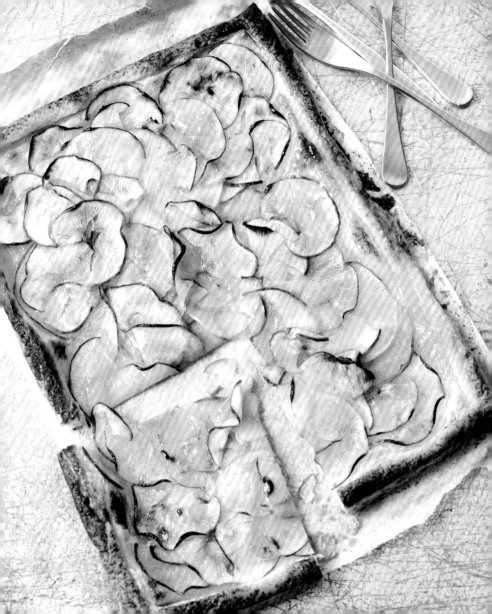

index

238

acknowledgments

Editorial Director Eleanor Maxfield
Assistant Editor Nell Warner
Senior Designer Jaz Bahra
Photographer William Shaw
Home Economist Denise Smart
Prop Stylist Cynthia Blackett
Production Manager Lisa Pinnell

240